TAKING A STAND

The Art, Science, & Practice of Resetting

MELANIE GRETSCH
LINDSEY STRASBERG
MELISSA LOWENSTEIN

WITH HOWARD GLASSER

Taking a Stand

The Art, Science, & Practice of Resetting

The Nurtured Heart Approach is a trademark of Nurtured Heart Publications. For information contact:

Nurtured Heart Publications
4165 West Ironwood Hill Drive
Tucson, Arizona 85745
E-mail: adhddoc@theriver.com

For information about bulk purchasing discounts of this book or other Nurtured Heart Approach books, CDs or DVDs and for orders within the book industry, please contact Brigham Distributing at 435-723-6611.

Cover Art by Alice Glasser.
Cover Design Alice Glasser and Owen Deleon
Book Design by Owen DeLeon - Owen Visual Communication

Editing by Melissa Lynn Lowenstein

Prolong Press Limited –Hong Kong

Library of Congress Card Catalogue Number: Pending

ISBN 978-1-64370-732-7

Printed in China
Second Printing: January 2019

TABLE OF CONTENTS

A NOTE
on Pronoun Use in this Book

In previous Nurtured Heart Publications books, we have attempted to adhere to traditionally gendered pronoun usage rules, using "He/him/his" or "She/her/hers" alternately when giving examples (or working through laborious constructions using "his or hers" or "she or he"). Over the past year, grammarians have given the green light to the use of "they/their/theirs" as a gender-neutral third-person singular pronoun. You will see this less traditional usage throughout this book.

This book is intended to support readers in a journey of self-help and self-discovery. It will not and is not intended to take the place of professional psychotherapy.

INTRODUCTION

We are parents of a total of seven children. Melanie has two; Lindsey has three; and Melissa has two (plus three stepchildren). Like all parents, our first parenting education came through our own diverse upbringings. We all recognized, at or before the moment when we held that first wailing newborn in our tired arms, that we'd probably benefit from some outside guidance in our efforts to parent effectively.

All of us, in our own ways, made mothering our most important research project. We read books and articles, attended classes, obtained coaching, and talked to other parents. In our combined half-a-century-plus of being mothers, we've all noticed that parenting advice tends to come in directly opposed dictates, such as:

Be the adult! Stay calm…no matter what!
vs.
Fully express emotions like anger, frustration and sadness when your kids' behaviors bring them up for you. They need to see how their actions impact others.

Set firm, consistent boundaries; don't bend the rules, ever.
vs.
Be sensitive to the individual needs of your kids and make accommodations for particular circumstances when rules are broken.

Build resiliency by letting children solve their own problems.
vs.
Always be there to guide and teach your children.

Don't interfere with sibling conflict.
vs.
Demand appropriate behavior within the family.

Every day, as parents, we navigate seemingly opposing "guidelines" like these. We are simultaneously worried about being too strict, which we are told will result in rebellious behavior; and being too lenient, which may jeopardize our children's health and well-being. And, like you, we also navigate our culture's and our communities' expectations around how children *should* behave and how parents *should* respond.

One saving grace for all of us has been in finding a parenting approach that offers a larger guiding structure that we can lean into when deciding how to respond to our children. This book will teach you about the approach we have found to be most effective: the Nurtured Heart Approach, which was developed in the late 1990s by psychotherapist Howard Glasser and is now in use in households, schools, and therapy practices all over the U.S. and in the UK, Australia, India, and other nations around the world.

The NHA is an elegant and intuitive model for interacting effectively with children in ways that help them become socially and emotionally healthy, and that reduces oppositional and defiant behaviors. Its simple foundational principles and practical guidelines resolve the kinds of contradictory advice described above.

All the authors of this book are certified trainers in the NHA, well-qualified to offer basic instruction about fundamentals of this approach and guidance about its application. Although many other helpful parenting approaches exist, the NHA has been a cornerstone of all our parenting journeys.

Another important saving grace has been our recognition that to make good parenting choices, we need to be present and connected to our own deepest intentions, instincts and wisdom. This can only happen if we are *emotionally regulated*. To practice the NHA successfully, especially with a challenging child or a particularly challenging behavior, requires emotional regulation: the ability to feel tough emotions like anger, fear, frustration, or even shame, and to be able to maintain one's cool enough to stick with the approach.

We all have our meltdown moments. No parent is immune. Think about how it feels when a child is on your last nerve. Feel that surge of emotion. What do you do in those moments? Do you yell and scream? Or do you disconnect? Withhold? Give the silent treatment? Say cruel things you would never say if you weren't over the top emotionally? Lecture? Threaten? Give warnings? Levy escalating consequences? Cave in to the child's demands in exchange for a few precious moments of peace, thus failing to enforce rules and support responsibilities? Resort to bribery?

Do these responses align with the parent you want to be? Your answer might be "yes" if you think that parenting is primarily about eliciting obedience. Or, maybe, like us, you have recognized that you want to be neither authoritarian nor permissive with your children, but that you want attunement, connection, and healthy limits. Like us, you may see the need for parenting in a way that supports your child's intrinsic drive toward harmony and cooperation – a way of relating to them that will organically lead to them wanting to relate and take responsibility in positive, age-appropriate ways. This book will guide you in this direction through the Nurtured Heart Approach, with a specific focus on helping parents hold to the tenets of this approach in the face of challenging behaviors and difficult situations.

We hope to give you useful information and space for reflection as you shift the way you parent – a primer on self-care and "self-parenting" that will give you an opportunity to look at your reactive triggers and to become more emotionally intelligent[1]. Learning to recognize these triggers when they come up and figuring out where they came from – usually, they date back to our own early childhoods and the ways we were parented – helps us to develop better self-control during decision-making moments with our children. These moments of recognition allow us to pause and make a conscious choice about how we respond.

This book isn't only for parents. All we share in these pages should prove helpful to therapists, educators, child care professionals, or youth providers – anyone who is invested in being at their best when interacting with children.

We came to this approach not to change our children, but to change ourselves; to take our self-care to a level that equips us to be the best parents we can be. If you're ready to take this journey yourself, let's begin.

---

[1]Emotional intelligence (EI or EQ) is the ability to perceive emotions, to access and generate emotions so as to assist thought, to understand emotions and emotional knowledge, and to reflectively regulate emotions so as to promote emotional and intellectual growth. (Mayer & Salovey, 1997)

CHAPTER ONE

A TALE
of Two Mothers

I'm in the shower, about to go to a Nurtured Heart Approach seminar in Los Angeles. My oldest daughter has been excruciatingly difficult all day, and I'm not handling it well. I'm standing under the hot spray, thinking all kinds of negative thoughts. I know I'm supposed to be energizing the positive, and I'm like, "how can I do that when there is clearly nothing positive here to energize?" … which turns into "F*** energizing positivity!"…which turns into "I hate this…" which then turns into "I am the worst. I am awful."

At that point, my child pokes her head in and asks to borrow something. I say "no." She walks away, mumbling, and I continue with my internal rant. I get out of the shower and bump into her in the hallway. And somehow, I manage to reach deep, deep down and find a small well of strength. I say, "I want to thank you for taking my 'no' to borrowing anything so well. You didn't curse, which shows that you really have so much strength and self-control."

"But, I did curse at you," she replies. "You just didn't hear me."

Deep breath. "Well then," I say, "thank you for saying it so softly that I couldn't hear you." And I walk away.

The moral of this story: All I knew was that I needed to find something positive to energize, although all I could see in that moment was the negative. As she poked her head into my shower, I was convinced that I had already failed. "I am the worst. I can't do this approach," I thought. But, then, when I bumped into her in the hallway, it was there. It was small. To many, what I came up with in that moment might be crazy; but it's what was there – that molecule of truth -- and I grabbed it. And by giving her that small dose of positivity, I not only changed the course of her day; I changed the course of my own day, too. I also know that with that grain of positive energy, I've just made a small deposit to the bank of her self-esteem and resiliency.

From your vantage point, this might seem like a minor victory. It might even seem nuts. I'm taking the long view, seeing each small success like this one as meaningful in shifting the way my daughter and I relate. Each one matters...a lot. Even if I can only find it in myself to create two or three moments like this a day, I know their impact adds up. Each moment where I feel reactive, angry, resentful, or hopeless – all feelings that come quite naturally and intensely to me, for reasons I'm about to disclose – and I can reset myself and show up in a positive way with my children...well, it feels like a pretty big victory to me. There is always something positive to energize—even when it's going poorly. And, by doing so, you reconnect with your child and you reset yourself. It's from this place that lasting changes are made.

My mother is schizophrenic. There's no easy way to talk about her, or the experience of being raised by her. She and my father divorced when I was three. My father remarried when I was five, and his new wife became a surrogate mother. I have two older sisters, Liz and Leslie, who were also surrogate mothers to me. I tried very hard to ignore my mother's role in my life. I tried hard to replace her. But, in the end, none of these surrogates could compensate for the reality of being parented by an un-medicated paranoid schizophrenic.

Looking back, I see how badly I wanted to pretend that my situation was not what it was. I pretended that my father's new wife was my mother. I pretended that my house was a normal house. I cleaned and polished it so that anyone coming over would only see a normal-looking home. I didn't want anyone to know how crazy it was inside. Cleaning was my only way to have a bit of control in that environment. I'd try to have the house smelling of products like Pledge, because in those commercials, I saw what I imagined to be a healthy, good home.

Her bedroom was complete madness. There was stuff everywhere. Magazines piled high, nothing thrown away. Bed unmade. Clothes piled all over. It was dark and oppressive. I would gather up my mother's belongings from around the house, open her door, and throw it all in there, and then I'd quickly shut the door again. This is how I dealt with my feelings about her, too – which is to say, I didn't deal with them much at all. I just kept storing them in a messy section of my heart.

I have so many strange memories with my mother. A few of them are sweet; I remember when I had a fever, she held me. Sometimes she would lie in her bed with me in the early mornings. Unfortunately, most of the memories are of being in a constant state of fight-or-flight. I was always either fighting against her or fleeing from her; running away, only to be dragged by her to our house again. It all felt normal to me: normal to have so much fear and anxiety; normal to have no one to talk to about it; normal to try to avoid conflict at all costs; normal to use my body as a receptacle for sad, angry feelings, with no knowledge of how to regulate my emotions. As a tween, I entered a new normal where I was often the one to start the conflict with her. I needed to fight it out to off-gas some of the anxiety and tension I carried around all the time. As I became a teenager, if I was angry, I yelled at her, or I fought with my sisters. I knew no other way to be with my family.

I was lucky that I had a lot of friends who took me in and took care of me. I slept at their houses all through the week. Their parents will always hold a dear place in my heart. On the weekends, I got to have visits with my father, a man with a big personality. He was, and still is, a bigger-than-life person. When he talked, my sisters and I were held in rapt attention. When he hugged me, I felt like my whole world was going to be okay.

Living with our mother, my two sisters and I were uprooted more times than I could count: every year, we moved into a new but smaller home. My oldest sister by six years left home as soon as she was old enough, which meant my other sister – older than me by three years – and I depended on each other all the time. We also fought all the time. I guess this was a way to disperse some of the energy stored inside us: it had to go somewhere.

A lot of parenting approaches tell us it is important to remain calm when dealing with a misbehaving child. How does a person *just be calm?* If you think it's simple or easy to do this, you aren't a reactive person. I wasn't taught any way to handle my feelings besides yelling, unloading, pushing, and fighting. I remember countless times when I was upset with my sisters and would take a room apart to show them just how wrong they were. It definitely got their attention. Even with my mother, sometimes, I'd start a fight with her just because it felt so good to unload my feelings. And, paradoxically, at some level, I recognized that fighting was the only reliable way to get connected with her.

And then, at 15, I moved in with my father. At first, I was so happy, but I didn't anticipate how lonely I would feel without the reactive exchanges with my mother. My father's work demanded constant travel; I was home alone (with a housekeeper, whose room was detached from the main house) often. My bottled-up feelings and too much time alone were a recipe for trouble. When I look back, the time living with my father obviously had more happy times than with my mother; but strangely, it also had much more sadness. I think it's because with my mother, at least I was expressed. I was not in doubt where I stood with her. We connected, even if that connection was often chaotic or terrifying. My father was always loving, and I always knew he loved me; but in his absence, I felt overwhelmed with fear that his love would go away.

By the time I hit my teenage years, I had so much rebellion in me, and I acted accordingly. No one knew what I was doing. I confessed everything to my father when I became an adult, and he was surprised to hear how destructive I had been. I told him that I had started drinking to find some respite from the pain and anxiety. In the Tennessee Williams play *Cat on a Hot Tin Roof,* the alcoholic character Brick talks about the "click" in his head that lets him know he's had enough to drink: "It's like a switch, clickin' off in my head. Turns the hot light off and the cool one on, and all of a sudden there's peace." I remember that feeling well. To the outside observer, I was a normal girl: sweet and kind. I don't think anyone was worried about me. Certainly, anyone who didn't know me well would never have seen me as a ticking time bomb.

My friends became my family. I hung out with kids who wanted to drink and to push the envelope. They were fun. They made me laugh. And, equally important, their parents didn't know where they were either.

We were fine hanging with each other any day of the week, sleeping over any night of the week. My anger grew, but my temperament seemed even, on the outside. Only rarely did I let my anger out anymore. My voice got more squeezed; it got smaller.

By a small miracle, I got into college. And thank God for college, because getting away changed my life. My freshman year, I continued not taking anything too seriously, but after my first semester, I realized that I wanted to do well in school. As school became important, I gained more confidence in myself. One teacher, Mr. Harvey, changed everything for me. I regularly came to his office with a long list of questions. He would say, "Sit down," as I walked in. He took the time to let me answer each question myself, and he didn't seem to mind how long it took me. Mr. Harvey had all the patience in the world, recognizing that I'd know it better if he didn't answer the questions for me.

For the first time in my life, I experienced attunement with an adult. He held "I know you can do this," and "I'll wait here until you see that you can do this," with great patience and respect towards me. Although he may have felt anxiety about the time I was taking or the information that I didn't understand – he may have felt it inside, having a long list of things to do himself – this was never communicated to me. By this way of being, he transmitted to me: *You matter. You are capable. You are worth my time and patience. You are worthy of respect.* This turned out to be one of my most important parenting lessons.

I met my husband at a weekend acting workshop. Many things drew us together, but one of the biggest was our mutual fear of abandonment. I had lived a relatively reactivity-free life since I had been out on my own, as I hadn't been in relationships intimate enough to stir that pot. Joel and I fought a lot, loudly and passionately, kind of like our lives depended on it, which they ultimately did. We were both fighting not to hurt, but to heal. We got help and found our way to a very calm place. There were always (and, frankly, still are) those odd moments where both of us are feeling so vulnerable and afraid that we explode on each other. Fortunately, we are at a place where we can step back after a short explosive time and say, "I am feeling this way because..." and the other can hear what, and why. And we find our way.

Joel was the first person in my life to sit there calmly while I was going off the rails. He'd say, "I'm just waiting until you are done, and then we can talk." No one had ever had that kind of compassion with me before. I learned to not be aggressive. I learned to talk about my feelings. I learned to not go peeling off in my car when I was angry. I learned to not push him when I was furious. Now, I might have a strong opinion, but unless something is really activated in me, this ugliness is gone. I have abandoned the notion that being angry means I am strong and in control. On the contrary: now, I know for certain that only when I find my way to a relatively neutral place can I respond well to something that is emotionally triggering.

So, here Joel and I were, in a pretty great place: both very emotional people with gaping psychic wounds who had learned to not be reactive with each other. We had learned to hear each other. We knew how to function in intimacy for the first time, trusting a partner with our hearts and souls.

And then we went and had a baby.

─┤ **LINDSEY** ├─────────────────────────────────

From the time I was an infant, I have lived with both chronic stress and acute fear stemming from serious health issues faced by my immediate family members. Although it's been challenging, these same challenges have brought me to a fierce appreciation for every day, every hug, and every precious moment of connection, laughter, and love.

I was an only child, born during final exams at the end of my dad's last year at USC Law School. Following his graduation, my mom and dad moved to San Diego, where he started work as an associate at a prestigious law firm. After having worked in Watts as a kindergarten teacher to put my dad through law school, my mom enjoyed her new role as a stay-at-home mom with her infant daughter.

One evening in December, when I was eight months old, my dad left his downtown office and got into his '65 Volkswagen Karmann Ghia to head home after a full day at work. As he passed the airport, he noticed cars ahead of him stopping quickly and slammed on his brakes. The driver behind him didn't notice the brake lights and smashed into the back of my dad's car at full speed.

Although my dad was wearing a seatbelt (not a given in the early 70's), his seat broke and his entire body slammed against the back window of the small car. My mom received a call from the California Highway Patrol telling her my dad had been in an accident and to come immediately to the hospital.

The emergency room doctors initially told my mom that my dad wouldn't make it through the night. His spinal cord was severed between his third and fourth cervical vertebrae. When the next morning came and he was still alive, they started lifesaving measures and surgeries that ultimately stabilized him.

During the next few months, I saw very little of my parents. I stayed with family friends while my mom stayed at the hospital around the clock. She would come visit me most days; some days, she would bring me to the hospital to visit my dad. While my dad hung upside down in a traction bed, I would crawl around on the floor underneath him and say "hi" (my first word). Just after my first birthday, my dad was moved to a rehabilitation facility where he lived for the next year.

The accident left my father a quadriplegic, paralyzed from the neck down. Although he was lucky enough to retain the function of one lung, which allowed him to breathe without a respirator, he was completely dependent on others. An electric wheelchair was his only form of mobility.

My mom went back to teaching to support our family while also being the sole caretaker for my dad and me. After my dad finished rehab, he went back to work at his law firm. The partners he worked for failed to give him any meaningful work assignments, so he opted to go out on his own as a sole practitioner. He maintained a successful, if modest, legal practice for over a decade.

I had two parents who adored me and made me feel important, and an extended family and network of family friends that provided extra support and warmth. Still, I was always afraid: that something worse would happen to my dad, or that something would happen to my mom and I would have to take care of myself and my dad. I was afraid of being yelled at or criticized by my parents who were using up every ounce of will power they had just to get through the day. I was afraid that someone would break into our house in the middle of the night, because my dad couldn't do anything to defend us; I was afraid that everyone out in public was looking at me and thinking I was weird because my dad was in a wheelchair.

As an only child, I didn't have anyone to share the intensity of my parents' daily existence: the weirdness of life with a paralyzed father. As I grew up, this was all my "normal," but it felt heavy, scary, and embarrassing. I used to look at able-bodied fathers and long to feel their strong arms and protective bodies pick me up, hold me, and keep me safe.

A week before my 13th birthday, my father ended up in a coma due to complications from his paralysis. Because his brain had been temporarily deprived of oxygen, my mom and the doctors determined that even if my dad woke up, he would have severe brain damage. My mom knew that my dad's wishes would be that she let him go, so we took my dad off life support the day after my 13th birthday.

Throughout high school and college, I moved through a sort of emotional fog that gave me a layer of insulation from my grief. I saw a therapist when I went home for the summers during college. With her help, I started to process my grief and to understand the emotional impact of my dad's injury and eventual death. I started to believe that I had the power to transform the places in me that were stuck and felt hopeless. Since then, I have been fortunate enough to find brilliant, wise therapists, coaches and teachers who have assisted me in my continuing passion to evolve and grow.

In my early 20's, having no real sense of where I was headed career-wise, I decided that a legal education would provide me with some direction and pedigree. Just before leaving California to go to law school at NYU, I met my future husband through a mutual friend.

David and I dated long-distance during my first year of law school. Toward the end of that first year, I was tempted to break things off with him. He had Type 1 diabetes and he wasn't taking great care of himself, which made me reluctant to head into a serious relationship with him. I told my mom, "I grew up with a paralyzed father…I don't want to knowingly walk into a life where I'm once again worrying about someone's health every day."

"You don't love someone to get a guarantee," she told me. "You just love them with all the risks that go along with that." The truth of her words took their rightful place in my psyche, and two months later, David and I were engaged. We married just before my third year of law school. While I have had a positive impact on David's health and self-care, there isn't a day that goes by that I don't have to accept that (a) I am not in control of how he chooses to take care of himself; (b) living with a loved one who has Type 1 diabetes is hard and sometimes scary; and (c) there's nothing I can do about (a) and (b).

I set out in my first three years practicing law to become a top entertainment lawyer. David and I came up with a five-year plan where I would work hard to make partner at my law firm, and then we would think about starting a family. About six months in, we went to a beach hotel in Puerto Rico. We were there with a bunch of young couples, one of which had a nine-month-old son. One afternoon, while we were hanging out at the beach, I looked over to see David holding the baby. I felt as though a bolt of lightning had hit me. Everything changed; suddenly, the five-year plan sounded ridiculous to me. I absolutely knew that we should have a baby RIGHT NOW – an insight I tried to explain to David on the plane on the way back to California. David took a little longer to come around, but 13 months later I was pregnant.

When I was pregnant with our first daughter, many wise friends suggested I go to therapy. "You have no relationship with your own mother...you need to go to therapy and discuss how you are feeling before you become a mother yourself," they'd say. High on pregnancy hormones, I would respond, "I'm feeling fine!"

In retrospect, I can see that I was tremendously anxious about becoming a parent, but I wasn't willing to acknowledge it. My anxiety made perfect sense: I had no model for the kind of mother I wanted to be. My own mother was so damaged, so incapable of loving me. Still, I thought I had done enough therapy already. I honestly believed I was ready, that I could step right up. The preeclampsia I suffered with that first pregnancy was, I believe, a direct result of the unacknowledged stress I felt about having my baby. I didn't rest enough. I didn't put my feet up enough. I wanted to prove that I didn't need much while pregnant. Remaining efficient and self-reliant helped me ignore my deeper, scarier feelings.

When I took my newborn home, I was afraid of being alone. I didn't want Joel to go anywhere. I wanted help but was afraid to have anyone else take care of her. I was embarrassed at needing help and yet, I wanted someone to be with me every day while I cared for my baby. I wanted my mother-in-law to stay with me. I was so afraid: that I'd hurt my daughter accidentally, that I'd do the wrong thing. I was afraid to be so intimate. I never had been. How do you do it? Everything about being a parent hurt my skin – hurt the very core of me. I felt more love for this little being than I could ever have imagined possible. I felt all the things I'd hoped I would feel, but I never expected to feel that depth of vulnerability.

I started to find a comfort in a rigid schedule – in

particular, a dependable and consistent nap schedule. If I could break the day down into parts, I was better. I had a sense of control. But when she wouldn't cooperate with my schedule, I felt a loss of control, and the fears would return.

I am terrified of flying. I feel, for the most part, like a whole functioning human being, but when I get on an airplane, I am just so sure we are going down. I have an irrational fear that grabs me and while intellectually, emotionally, I know that I am safe, I feel completely stuck, as though I am going to die *right now*. And, for most of my life, flying was the one place that could conjure this complete, out-of-control vulnerability – until I had a baby. Suddenly, I was confronted with the feeling that this relationship had the power to end me. I fly once or twice a year, but my kid is with me daily. And while I'd like to get over my fear of flying, I can white-knuckle through it because I do it so seldom; but I *had* to work through these feelings with my daughter. She was the first thing to enter my life that brought me to resolve to do whatever it took to be better, to heal. For the first time, I was willing to deal with my unresolved feelings about my own mother.

I came to realize that I would not consider this life worth anything if I didn't become the kind of mother I had dreamed of being. My relationship with my child (and, later, children) became the single most important thing in my life.

LINDSEY

I loved everything about being pregnant. I read books, took birth classes, did prenatal yoga, and got prenatal massages, all with the idea that I'd like to give birth without pain medications if possible. The labor and birth process turned out to be all I had dreamed of and more. I found strength and resilience that I didn't know I possessed. Feeling my baby's body move through me as I gave birth, I felt powerful, unbridled, euphoric and fearless. In those moments, I felt connected to my mother, my grandmothers, and a long line of female ancestors.

I had always been overly reliant on intellect and analysis in my life. After the transformational experience of labor and birth, I was more confident that my instincts and intuition would guide me as a mother. There were the typical new-parent insecurities and difficulties in that first year, but I also had a deep-rooted belief in my ability to figure it all out. Apparently, I was determined to prove this point: I had three children in under four years. For a few months, we were buying three different sizes of diapers!

I was so taken by the pregnancy and childbirth experience that I would have gladly kept going and had four children. David, however, was convinced that we had our hands plenty full with three. As it turned out, he was right. When our son and youngest child was a mere 10 months old, he was diagnosed with Type 1 diabetes – just like his dad.

MELANIE

I remember the first time I felt my reactivity leak out onto my baby. She was a year old. As I walked her in the living room to get her to sleep, she kept taking her pacifier out of her mouth and dropping it on the floor. I'd pick it up and give it back to her and she'd throw it again. She thought this was the *best* game.

I began to get aggravated but kept picking up the pacifier and giving it back to her. Then, a wave of anger rose in me. I picked up her pacifier and threw it far into the other room. It was small as far as reactive moments go, but I remember the feeling of not being able to control my response. I realized I had just acted in a way I could not control. However small it had been, I'd just done something that had no edit—no lid.

I learned to relax and revel in the time with my kids when things were predictable and I could count on their responses; but when things went out of the box, the chaos in my DNA would be stirred. Reading parenting books helped to keep me righted, so I read them constantly. That's when I found the Nurtured Heart Approach. When I read *Transforming the Difficult Child*, the first book written about the NHA, I saw immediately how it would help me be a better parent. It showed me a true method for handling 'off' behavior, as well as for celebrating the greatness of my kids. It gave me such a clear way through the maze.

Part of what the Approach teaches is how to be aware of the many moments when a child is not breaking rules – which, even for the most misbehaving child, is most of the time. As I directed this awareness back at myself and saw the many moments where I was *not* reactive, I felt proud of myself and happy. The happier and prouder I was, the more I learned to control myself. And the more I saw my kids flourish, the more it helped me too.

The Nurtured Heart Approach taught me that nothing changes your energy as much as finding something good in what your kid has done, especially in that moment when you think, "I can't do it. I can't find anything good to say!" But then, you muster the strength to compliment the child, like I did that day in the shower. "Even though you were yelling, you didn't curse." (I think our grandparents would call this crazy parenting.) "I want you to know how much I appreciate that, and how that shows your greatness in your ability to control yourself." (Even if you were thinking that the child was out of control, you find the place she *did* use some control, and you celebrate that step forward!)

After you find whatever nugget of positivity you can grasp in that moment where you might otherwise spiral into negativity, you are left with your own soul, intact.

Your relationship with your kid is also intact. And now, you can actually parent, guide and teach, because a child will listen to a sane person, and I am here to testify that *no one listens to an insane person.*

─── LINDSEY ─────────────────────────────────────

Having an infant diagnosed with a chronic disease continued a lifelong pattern of living with health issues in my family. I had already brought a level of vigilance and fear to my parenting as a result of the stressful and sometimes downright scary ups and downs of living with a paralyzed father and then a new husband with Type 1 diabetes. My son's diabetes diagnosis started off with a trip to the emergency room and four-day hospital stay. Once we took him home, we started on a daily regime that included 10-12 shots of insulin, 8-10 finger stick blood tests, and constant insulin dose calculations and blood glucose charting. My fear had a new focus.

David and I had very different reactions to the stress and fear involved in caring for an infant with diabetes. I fantasized that my attention to detail and constant care could bring about perfect blood glucose levels; I was quickly disabused of this notion as I learned that mimicking a pancreas is beyond the skill of even the best-intentioned parent or caregiver. David was on guard to make sure I didn't overreact and smother our son. Three years later, our son was also diagnosed with celiac disease. So, in addition to our constant monitoring of his blood glucose and insulin doses, we also had the task of tracking ingredients and possible cross-contamination in anything he might eat. It became an ongoing internal battle to not give myself over to the hyper-vigilance and anxiety I had been living with all my life.

I knew from the beginning that parenting would

be a constant path of evolution for me. Aside from the challenge of having a chronically-ill child, I experienced the button-pushing characteristic of every parent-child relationship. Each child seemed designed to push a different set of buttons.

We enrolled in a progressive preschool, Crestwood Co-op Nursery School, where the emphasis on parent education gave me a foundation based in the best research in child development. While at Crestwood, I met Melanie when our children were in the toddler group together. We soon learned that we shared a passion for personal growth and transformation, especially in the parenting arena. Melanie had a knack for sifting through Internet resources to identify parenting books that stood out. If she liked something, she would encourage me with loving persistence until I finally found the time to read the books she recommended. Two such books changed my parenting life forever: *Scream-Free Parenting* by Hal Edward Runkel and *Transforming the Difficult Child* by Howard Glasser.

Scream-Free Parenting was the first resource that brought my attention squarely to the fact that changing my own behavior was the most important aspect of changing parenting patterns that weren't working. Although the title initially dissuaded me because I don't do a lot of literal screaming at my kids, I ended up learning that I had my own versions of "screaming." *Scream-Free* points out that anything we do from a space of reactivity, where we are emotionally triggered, has the same impact as screaming. I learned that kids *will* throw down the gauntlet of a challenging behavior to see whether the adults in their lives will pick it up and be reactive, and that if I can just not do that, I step into being the kind of parent I want to be.

When Melanie introduced me to the Nurtured Heart Approach, everything fell into place. Here was an approach that not only focused on my patterns of behavior, but also gave me a lens through which to see my children as whole, dynamic and powerful individuals who are in the process of recognizing and harnessing their greatness.

CHAPTER TWO

AN INTRODUCTION TO
the Nurtured Heart Approach

Psychotherapist Howard Glasser first developed the Nurtured Heart Approach in the 1990s. He was having little success supporting families with difficult children using the traditional approaches he learned in his training as a therapist. He began to intuit a new way of working with the energetic connection between adults and children. His experimentation led him to develop an approach that, for some time, didn't have a specific name or a place within any existing psychotherapeutic category. What it did have was an unprecedented level of impact. Difficult, oppositional, distractible, defiant children were coming around to positive behaviors and intrinsic motivation.

Word got out, and Howard began to build a reputation for being able to cure ADHD. In his city (Tucson, Arizona), the therapeutic community began to clamor for him to offer training in his method. He resisted, because he couldn't see himself getting up in front of a crowd to present his ideas – and because, as well as his ideas were working to help his clients, he feared getting laughed out of the room because they were so off the beaten track.

Finally, he agreed to do a small training. A few weeks later, someone who had been there approached him in the grocery store. He told Howard that the material he'd been taught had been incredibly effective for both himself and his agency. The participant was so enthusiastic and grateful that Howard recognized that he was being called to keep refining his methods and training others to use them. He further refined the approach, gave it a name, and founded a counseling center, the Center for the Difficult Child, where he worked with families and children. At the Center, interns he trained in his Nurtured Heart Approach had better results than those achieved by seasoned therapeutic veterans using more traditional approaches. Since then, he has written several books about the Approach and founded the Children's Success Foundation (www.childrenssuccessfoundation. com), which is dedicated to helping adults build transformative and deeply nurturing relationships with children in their care. He eventually left his therapy practice to develop and write about the approach and to offer trainings.

A decade and a half later, *Transforming the Difficult Child*, Howard's first book on the NHA (coauthored with fellow therapist Jennifer Easley), remains a top-selling title on ADHD at Amazon. com. In week-long Certification Training Intensives in cities around the world, Glasser and co-trainers teach the approach in depth to parents, educators, therapists, and school administrators, many of whom then go on to teach others in classes and trainings in their home cities. All in all, the NHA's influence has spread to hundreds of thousands of people: adults and youth in public schools (including a growing number of educational implementations of NHA district-wide), foster care agencies, therapeutic schools and centers, and individual households just like ours.

If you're like us, the best proof of any approach's effectiveness is its actual impact within your own home and relationships – so let's get you started with a brief overview of the basics. To read inspiring testimonials and research results, go to www.childrenssuccessfoundation.com. For a more comprehensive introduction to the Approach, consult any of the other books (available at Amazon.com or at the Children's Success Foundation web site) or take the free introductory e-course offered at the CSF site.

PARENTING YOURSELF TO BETTER PARENT YOUR CHILD

At its foundations, the Nurtured Heart Approach is not about changing children's behavior; it is about changing the ways we relate to children. The shifts in behavior that occur in the child being nurtured through this approach come through this transformed relationship, which sometimes requires significant internal change for the adults in the picture.

Parenting our own children well has required that we learn ways of relating that our own parents did not have access to, but that are now understood to be ideal in the context of the parent-child relationship. Most people parenting now didn't learn these skills implicitly – as an integrated part of their relationships with their own parents – so some awareness, work, and practice are required. Not only does this method give tools for parenting our children; it also provides guidelines that help us to 're-parent' ourselves. The Nurtured Heart Approach enables us to give ourselves a corrective experience of self-parenting to help us be the kind of parents we wish to be to our children.

MELANIE

Because of my upbringing, I have always had to take care of myself and walk myself through difficult situations. From a very young age, I can remember talking soothingly to myself as though I were a parent comforting a child. Now, as a parent, I still self-parent. I talk myself through the act of letting go of control and constantly search for the willingness to face my fears.

In the end, it's up to parents to do the work they need to do to be level and regulated, no matter the difficulties of our parenting circumstances. We cannot expect our children to learn to self-regulate if we cannot do so ourselves. So, every day, in the face of childhood conditioning that makes me vulnerable to losing it, I parent myself first so that I can parent my children as calmly and levelly as possible.

I had a therapist once say to me, "The only way to stay calm is to make it the most important priority. No matter what's coming at you, stay calm. *Whatever you have to do*, stay calm." For a time, when my kids would yell at each other, I felt like Rain Man, repeating to myself, "The only thing that matters is staying calm...the only thing that matters is staying calm." I am convinced that for those of us who are reactively challenged, this is the only way through.

I can also remember the day when it hit me like a revelation: *My kids can lose it, but I cannot.* The only one I truly can control in this dynamic is my own self, which means I can hold myself accountable 100% of the time. Of course, I will lose it now and again, because we all do, but I still hold myself accountable to return to balance as quickly as possible. I also hold myself accountable for when I feel overwhelmed or annoyed. Even though, in those moments, I haven't yet lost it, I know that if I let myself feel this way for any length of time, I will lose it soon – so I'd better go take care of myself (reset) by breathing, talking to my husband or Lindsey, writing, meditating, yoga, exercise, or seeing my therapist.

IMPROVEMENT VS. TRANSFORMATION

By design, the Nurtured Heart Approach goes beyond simple behavioral improvement. Rather than having a goal of modifying the child's behavior, its intention is to transform the relationship between you and your child; and to then, through that transformed relationship, motivate and inspire the child to relate to everything in their world in a more positive way. The Approach shifts the very same intensity that has gone awry into fuel for the life force that propels the child's greatness. A significant side benefit is the transformation it creates in you, the adult learning and applying the approach.

The key to this transformation is the building of *inner wealth*.

Through the withholding of energetic exchange around negativity and through direct experiences of being honored, appreciated and recognized, the child has a lived experience of being deeply seen. The adult has the experience of deep gratitude for the absence of misbehavior and for every small increment of desired behavior. Inner wealth – a sense of being valuable and great, right now, today, without any hoops to jump through or high expectations to meet – becomes the medium for transformation for both child and parent. At some point, the child no longer feels the impulse to act out as often. They become more content and self-motivated to be in relationship in progressively positive ways. Instead of acting out negatively, they act out greatness.

Most children feel most seen when they are pushing boundaries and breaking rules, because that is when adults most reliably show up, and where they show up with the greatest energy and intensity. When a child is well-behaved, adults tend not to make much of a fuss. If the child is simply doing what is expected, adults are likely to go about their business without acknowledging them; if the child does something positive, they might get a "Good job!" or a "Nice work!" but rarely get feedback that matches the intensity they can easily elicit from even approaching the breaking of a rule.

A child can go for quite some time being "good" without getting much in the way of intense, energized, or deeper connection with caregivers. Most of us learned that a responsible parent is supposed to jump in to correct, teach, and guide when things are going wrong. Usually, the moment rules are broken or boundaries pushed, adults bring sweet exhortations, warnings, threats, high-energy lectures, pep talks, frustrated reactivity, or other energized interactions and interventions designed to steer the child back toward being "good." Although some of these interventions feel better than others – certainly, a pep talk ("I just *know* you can do better! Come on!") or sweet exhortation (with hugs and affection: "Sweetheart, I know you're tired, but I need you to stop whining right now") feels better than a lecture, warning, threat, or punishment – in the end, they all read the same to the child: *Misbehavior is a reliable way for me to "get"* what Glasser refers to as "the gift of YOU."

The result is a kind of "upside-down energy" where the child feels inexorably drawn to break rules or be oppositional to garner the connection they crave. The NHA turns this dynamic right-side-up to give the child a consistent lived experience of being seen and acknowledged in their greatness. It literally makes this experience impossible to avoid by turning our awareness to the fact that our children make many positive choices every day – choices to which we were all but oblivious in the past. When we start noticing all the things our children do right every day, our perspective on our children is transformed. It becomes natural and joyful to acknowledge their many facets of greatness daily.

The transformative factor with this approach is the child feeling their greatness shining from within and having a consistent experience of that greatness being recognized. Eventually, the child becomes intrinsically greatness-oriented, developing a kind of inner GPS that guides them to living the highest good of who they really are – the goodness of their true self.

NURTURED HEART Contentions and Intentions

The NHA rests upon a few 'intentions' and 'contentions' designed to awaken parents to the ways in which children respond to the energies of interaction and how 'normal methods' might be unintentionally promoting problematic behaviors in their children. They are illustrated with simple stories that contain wisdom to help shift these patterns, and they help to explain the actual Stands and techniques described later in this chapter.

Toys R Us

Which, of the many toys you've bought for your child, do you think is their favorite?

What if it were...YOU?

It's obvious, if you think about it. Can you think of any other toy that has as many features, as much variety, and as much potential for rewarding interaction as you: the adult? Most children discover very early in life that this favorite toy's most lively and animated features are most readily accessible via their negative choices.

In the Nurtured Heart Approach, we operate with a core belief that children's misbehavior, rule-breaking or boundary pushing are almost always, to some extent, about trying to connect with us, the most important people in their lives.

| MELANIE |

When my oldest daughter was eight years old, she used to start a lot of arguments in the morning before school. I remember the day that I had an "aha" moment where I recognized that her motive in starting these arguments was to connect with me.

On that morning, I came into the kitchen. she stood at the light switch, turning the light on…and off…and on…and off again. I asked her to stop. She wouldn't. On, off, on, off. I could feel my anger start—after all, I had asked her to stop, and she had ignored me.

But then, I got crystal clear. She was trying to get me to react, and the more I said, "Stop it," the more interesting the interaction became for her. "Can I turn you on and off like a switch, Mommy?" she seemed to be asking.

Think about it. When a child receives a new toy, they try all its features. When they find features that are interesting, they'll return to them. More boring features will be ignored after a few tries. Features that are interesting some of the time – especially if they're REALLY interesting, with lots of sounds and visuals, and if they're different each time they do respond – will merit frequent returns: will it do that thing *this* time? Will it do something even more noisy, emotional or dramatic? *Hmmm, if I edge near breaking this rule today, when my favorite toy seems like it's in a good mood, it does one thing…if I do it on a day when it's in a lousy mood, it does something entirely different!*

Scary? Maybe, a little. Fascinating? Full of drama? For sure. And for an intense child, the fascination and drama trump the fear. The need for intense connection outweighs concern about whether the toy might come out swinging.

It can be hard not to take personally the button-pushing our children do to get their favorite toys to dance. This Toys R Us concept has helped us see that they aren't out to get us; they don't hate us; and – even in the case of our tweens and teens – they haven't stopped caring about us. They are, even in their worst moments, trying to get more connected and engaged with us, albeit through a route of negativity.

MELANIE

While my eight-year-old flipped the light switch despite my protestations, I stepped back. Not just in my mind: I literally took a step backward. Then, instead of engaging with her directly around the behavior I wanted her to stop, I walked away.

It wasn't easy. I wanted to correct and admonish her. Instead, I went into my room and I breathed. I disengaged from her instead of diving into the relationship when she was doing what I didn't want her to do. Instead of giving her my energy in response to her negative choice, I took a moment to do some self-care. I reset myself.

There was a tentative knock at my door. "Yes?" I called. She came into the room and hugged me and said, "I am so sorry!"

Although at the time, we didn't call what had happened a 'reset,' that is what we each had done: reset ourselves. In response to my choice to reset, she had reset herself. We were starting fresh, in a positive space. Instead of diving into a battle with her, I had given her room to remember herself and seek me out in a different way.

All kids, especially the challenging ones, are looking for deep connection and stimulation. Even if it seems counterintuitive, consider yourself among their most important sources of that connection and stimulation. Just trust us on this point and proceed as if it is true. If you're able to do this, the proof that you are your child's favorite toy will make itself evident soon enough. This approach wouldn't work if you weren't.

Being your child's favorite toy may feel like a very big responsibility, but it's one that comes with power. You can purposefully use this relationship to move your child into discovery of their greatness.

Some parents or caregivers feel resistant to the use of the Toys R Us analogy regarding children who have endured trauma or adverse experiences. It can, at the outset, feel minimizing of the impact of a child's very real early life challenges. This issue is addressed in depth in Chapter Five; refer especially to the boxed section on pages 130-133 if it is already coming up for you.

$100 BILLS FOR NEGATIVITY

Imagine that every time your child misbehaved, you handed them a crisp $100 bill and told them, "Stop misbehaving!" No one would, of course, dream of giving a child a $100 bill for making a poor choice; still, this is, fundamentally, how the child perceives receiving an energetic connection in response to rule-breaking. Even if it comes in the form of anger or punishment, the child perceives it energetically as a reward, especially if the *absence* of bad behavior is met with little more than a low-key "Good job!" or with no acknowledgement at all. If little or no connection is available in return for *not* making trouble, children will opt for whatever they can get...by misbehaving.

| MELANIE |

Not giving $100 bills for negativity is sometimes counterintuitive. Recently, my daughter was running late. She had a school performance. When we got in the car and Joel saw the time, he commented, "You are going to be so late" (a source of anxiety for him), which made her lose it. In the depths of a meltdown, she kicked and screamed.

Our tendency is to want to start lecturing and moralizing about being late or about her meltdown; this time, we gave her some space to yell for a few moments and stayed quiet. Within minutes, she began to stop and reset herself. After a bit of quiet from her, we both celebrated her ability to reset.

If you don't know the Nurtured Heart Approach, the natural question here is: how can you not parent her (correct her) through the bad behavior? Two important things occurred in that car that originated not in parental dictates or lectures, but in her own movement toward emotional honesty and self-control: one, she became overwhelmed with anxiety at the thought of being late; and two, she was able to calm herself down from that attack. Knowing what we know from the NHA, we could see this not as an opportunity to correct our daughter, but as an opportunity to witness her managing her own emotions and bringing herself back to a calmer, more balanced place. Our job, then, became one of holding up a mirror reflecting her in that moment of strength, showing her the incontrovertible truth of her own power.

Ask yourself, which approach to that meltdown would you want your kid to think about for the rest of the day? Which one will teach her about herself? Which one will deepen your bond and deepen her sense of source? Not giving her the $100 bill allowed her to reset herself and allowed all of us to stay connected. What may have happened in the past is one or both parents would start lecturing, which would augment the meltdown; as our own anxiety rose, we would start to yell; everyone would say things they would later regret; and parents and child would spend the day feeling awful.

I see this in my relationship with my kids. I give $100 bills for negativity all the time. I know better. I live NHA and deeply love it; and, yet, many times in a day or a week, I concede. I always need to stay conscious and aware to avoid energizing and reinforcing the negative connections, make quick turnarounds, and repair where needed. I want both my girls to be rich in positivity and confidence, not rich in negativity!

Begin to tune in during your interactions with your child. Notice where your energy naturally wants to go. Notice whether you feel relatively disengaged when everything's fine, and notice how much you want to lean in, initiate conversation, correct, or otherwise intervene at the first hint of a problem. Notice whether, when problems arise, you feel drawn in, as though you've been hooked. Recognize that you have a choice about when to lean in and connect. As you catch yourself engaging with negativity, don't blame yourself! This reflects the normal, traditional ways to parent – even the so-called "positive parenting" approaches many of us learned. Conventional methods are inherently reactive to negative behaviors. We're all just trying as hard as we can with the methods we've had at our disposal.

Nurtured Heart Approach is a truth-based approach. If a child looks like they are going to melt down but haven't, what's the truth of the moment? It's that they haven't. Anything else is a story — no matter what your past experience or your perception of what is most likely to happen next.

This recognition sets you squarely in an advantageous position. Don't let it pass by — dive in. It's time to "play hardball" (as Howard Glasser likes to say): to give credit for every ounce of good decision-making that child is doing in this moment. Whether they are deciding *not* to fall apart, *not* to fly off the handle, *not* to argue, or *not* to hit someone, the bottom line is that when you attend to the truth of this moment, you create space for great celebration and appreciation.

We are so willing to dive in when the nonsense is transpiring — in the midst of the falling-apart, flying-off-the-handle, arguing, and hitting. Why not give credit for the self-control needed to show restraint? For the demonstration of power required to reel one's self in when there is a deep temptation to say or do things that would have crossed a line?

If you want to be a warrior, dial in the truth of the moment. Don't default to the tendency to leave the present moment, to get caught up in the fear of a problem or anticipation of an issue. As soon as we do that, we surrender our power to make a difference.

What follows are three intentions of the Nurtured Heart Approach that can serve your cause of dialing in this warrior version of the truth.

THE DANCING TOLL TAKER

When we are no longer able to change a situation, we are challenged to change ourselves.
— Viktor Frankl, neurologist, psychologist, and Holocaust survivor

In the NHA books and trainings, Howard tells a story about a tollbooth attendant on the San Francisco Bay Bridge. The person who initially told the story shared that he saw one attendant dancing in his booth, and so chose to pull into that lane to investigate. No other attendant looked nearly as happy to be on the job. When asked about this, the dancing toll taker exclaimed that he had the best job in the world – that he could hardly believe he was being paid to enjoy amazing views, talk to kind drivers, and practice his dancing. "But the other attendants don't seem to see it that way," said the driver, and the dancing toll taker replied, "Oh, those guys in the stand-up coffins? They're no fun!"

This story illustrates that we all have a choice about the way we see things. To stick with the toll taker metaphor, we can choose to focus on the traffic, the noise, the rude drivers, or other less positive aspects of our circumstances; or we can choose to see ways in which the job at hand is a privilege and to openly celebrate and reinforce what we love about it.

Howard is fond of saying that it isn't even a glass-half-full/half-empty question – it's about the beautiful glass we are privileged to hold; the fact that we have working hands to grasp things with; the fact that we are here, today, in this moment, surrounded by blessings that can awaken profound gratitude. There needn't be anything at all in the glass to access a great attitude. We are only limited by the openness of our minds, heart, and imaginations. The Nurtured Heart Approach is about making a point of noticing these blessings as often as possible, and using our creativity to become appreciatively aware of blessings that might not otherwise be evident.

MELANIE

When we first started NHA, I remember my husband saying, "I had no idea how much good our daughter does every day." This had always been true of her, but until we started focusing on the good, all we could see was how much she was doing wrong: *stop fighting with your sister! Chew with your mouth closed! Pick up your clothes! Get off your phone, get off your phone, get off your phone!*

Once we made the choice to shift our perspectives, together my husband and I would take stock of all the things done right: the smile, the laugh, the conversation, the amazing thing she said, the picture drawn, the connection to friends, the run she went on, the kiss, the dish on the counter, the on-time to school, the doing homework without being asked.

And still, I get into periods of correcting and trying to change and control my kids. I realize that when I parent from this vantage point, I am not enjoying my children.

Our connection, in those moments, is about correction and control, about letting them know what they didn't do right. If that's all I am communicating, it's no wonder they don't enjoy me. The way they respond to me in those moments proves the rule: that true connection and enjoyment happen in positivity, and that the best kind of growth and learning happen where true connection and enjoyment are in play.

Our responses to bad behavior, or even the *threat* of bad behavior, tend to be far more energized than anything we do in response to its absence. And technically, any time a child is *not* breaking rules, she is doing innumerable things right. *That's* when to lean in.

BABY STEPS / MIRACLES FROM MOLECULES

Think of a baby taking its first steps. Do you respond to the wobbling, falling, and trying again of an adorable toddler with criticism or negative judgment? Of course not! You respond with joy, wonder, and enthusiasm at every tiny movement toward walking.

We lose appreciation for baby steps as our children grow. Try to restore it now. Begin to see success in every moment where nothing bad is happening. Revisit the sense of wonder that filled your heart when you watched your own child take their first step. Bring this wonder to your interactions with your child today, whatever their age.

If you're great at making mountains from molehills – building small dramas into big problems – you'll also be great at making *miracles from molecules:* seeking out success in everyday moments and choices. A child who gets to school on time, for example, is making many good choices that demonstrate discipline, positive effort, and self-care. A parent who gets themselves to work on time is making the same kinds of good choices!

Before recognizing that this was a choice we could make, we could talk for days about the kids not putting their dishes in the sink – and when they *did* put their dishes in the sink, we barely noticed. Seeing and commenting on the microscopic good choices feels so much better than picking at the microscopic bad choices.

We are so quick to recognize when *not-great* happens, and so explicit in our commentary. Consider: How not-great would it be if your child broke a rule right now? And how great is it, then, that they aren't? Now is the time to fully feel this gratitude and recognize it with generosity. Begin to see that when your child chooses not to act out or break rules, it is exactly that: a choice – one that can be celebrated. We are so profoundly talented at seeing tiny slivers of what's wrong. It's time to put that same talent to use seeing all the enhanced levels of good and great. Begin to get comfortable with gratitude for the absence of all the not-great things that *could* be transpiring. How great is it that those problems *aren't* happening? How great is it that you can enrich your child's life and your relationship with them by calling them out for all the character it takes to be in that mode?

TIME-IN / VIDEO GAME PARENTING

Think about your favorite sport. When a player violates a rule and earns a time-out, the true motivation to sit patiently through that time-out is the knowledge that the thrill of returning to play is on the other side of that penalty. In video games, breaking a rule or making a mistake leads to a temporary bump from play or the game ending – another version of time-out – but all the player needs to do is wait a few moments to start it up again.

In both the sporting event and the video game, the time-out/reset is simple and clear. Oops! Broke a rule; time-out. Endure a brief, low-energy time-out, and it's time-in again: scoring, engaging with teammates, the thrill of competition and the movement toward scoring more points and levels of attainment.

Both sports and video games are famously engaging activities even for the child with overwhelming intensity. The reason for this goes back to the clear, predictable, and positively-weighted energetic relationship each creates between time-in and time-out. No lectures, scolding, long-winded explanations, or comforting are called for when the player is sitting on the penalty bench or re-starting another round

The Three Stands of the Nurtured Heart Approach

First Stand: ABSOLUTELY NO!

I will not energize negativity.

(By "negativity," we mean any behavior that we do not wish to see more of.)

When I feel drawn to give my energy, connection and relationship to the child in response to unwanted behaviors, I will reset myself, and then I will respond in accordance with the Second Stand:

Second Stand: ABSOLUTELY YES!

I will relentlessly energize positivity – including any area in which negativity is not being expressed in this moment.

(Positivity, here, defines any behavior and character that we do wish to see and encourage.)

Third Stand: ABSOLUTELY CLEAR!

I will give an un-energized, non-relational, non-punitive consequence (a reset) every time a rule is broken. I will have crystal clarity around the rules, and unless the line is crossed, I will return to ABSOLUTELY YES – reinforcing any choice to not break a rule.

of their online game. It's a moment's pause. The player knows what rule was broken, and is now primarily motivated by the excitement of time-in. It's a no-brainer to reset to wanting to play their best and to jump back in the game as soon as they are allowed…and to channel any frustration they're feeling about having broken a rule into staying in play and achieving next levels of greatness.

THE THREE STANDS AND THE RESET:
AN INTRODUCTION

So: the goal here is not improvement, but transformation; and the keys to transformation lie in the Three Stands, which provide the Approach's guiding structure. An integral part of these Stands is a magical, challenging, and liberating thing Glasser calls the *reset*.

As you can see, the Approach involves two distinct types of reset. The third-stand reset is the one given to a child in response to a broken rule. The first-stand reset is the *self-reset*. It's what you do to regulate yourself whenever your own reactivity threatens to interfere with your ability to disengage around negativity – when you feel tempted to give yourself, your energy, your heart, or your words to something you *don't* want. It's how you calm yourself enough to return to "absolutely no" (the First Stand) and "absolutely yes" (the Second Stand).

The self-reset asks that we develop awareness and skills that will enable us to:

- Recognize when we need a self-reset.
- Respond to that need with a pause and a return to higher intention.
- Take the self-reset over the reflexive drive to indulge in an explosion of temper, a bout of sulking, an attempt to exert control, a passive-aggressive retort, a lecture, or any of the other avenues we have all taken in our efforts to impact the outcome of an uncomfortable interpersonal situation.
- Fully feel uncomfortable emotions and sensations long enough to let them flow through you or be redirected rather than acting out habitual reactive patterns.
- Refuse to give any energy, connection or relationship to perceived or real negativity.
- Jump in with appreciation and purposeful recognition as soon as rules are no longer being broken.

When a kid is being difficult and you are at the end of your own rope, it doesn't usually end well unless you reset into a non-reactive, non-oppositional space – or, in a pinch, pretend to do so (more on this later in this chapter). If the child knows your goat is gotten, the negativity continues, and the two of you are caught in a familiar and unproductive dance. With practice, you'll learn to handle negative energy and acting-out like a practitioner of aikido, a martial art where you go *with* and utilize the force coming at you instead of against it. You'll develop the skill to redirect that energy rather than fighting it.

This self-reset is especially magical when you perform it in front of your child/ren. When they see you getting ready to lose your cool, and then they see you regain control and act according to your higher intentions instead, they see an example of power and clarity that they will want to emulate.

It can feel impossible to find the positive thing to acknowledge in what feels like a sea of dysfunction. Sometimes it can feel wrong to even try. What we'll ask of you is that you keep trying to dig deep enough to move away from the judgment and take the reset: to change your energy to change your child's.

THE FIRST STAND: ABSOLUTELY NO!
REFUSAL TO ENERGIZE NEGATIVITY

This Stand is about refusing to allow your child to make you, their favorite toy, blink, whirr, hop, screech, or otherwise respond when they are doing something you don't want them to do. It is about practicing a self-reset any time you feel compelled to unwittingly give the gift of yourself in response to what you don't want.

This is *not* about refusing to meet the basic needs of an infant or very young child. We're not suggesting that you deny connection to a pre-verbal child who is crying or acting out because they need food, love, or comfort. This Stand only applies once a child reaches a developmental stage where they begin to do things that don't seem connected to any kind of survival needs. It's also not about ignoring bad behavior. Ignoring rule-breaking leads to escalation. Refusal to energize negativity, combined with a commitment to energize positive behavior and give resets every time rules are broken, is the transformative combination. Combine both these Stands with a commitment to give an un-energized consequence every time a line is crossed, and you have a new collaborative energy that is life-changing for all involved.

Take, for example, the standard tantrum. Mom is in the kitchen with her three-year-old son. He spots a box of cookies on the counter and wants one; he hasn't had lunch, so Mom says no. The child escalates into a full-blown tantrum. Now, Mom has a few choices in terms of her response. She can try to talk him out of or distract him from the tantrum, cave in and give him the cookie, try to hold and comfort him, yell at him or threaten punishment, or try to ignore the screeching, kicking, and angry language until he wears himself out.

If Mom responds to this meltdown in accordance with Stand 1, she won't allow herself to indulge any impulse to try to squash down, comfort away, or otherwise meet the child's tantrum energy with the gift of herself. She'll go about her business – not in the sense of ignoring the child but paying keen attention toward the child without the child catching on that she's doing so. She is present and watching out for the child's safety, but she is not interacting directly with the child around the unwanted behavior. Although she might feel irritation, worry, concern, or anger, she does not reveal these emotions to the child. Crucially, she resets the child any time rules are being broken (Stand 3), all the while directing her energy toward resetting herself as many times as necessary to adhere to Stand 1 and avoid energizing the unwanted behavior.

Resetting the child – which you will learn about in detail in the section on Stand 3 – requires that she watch like a hawk for the child's smallest movement towards de-escalation. Wherever she sees that, Stand 2 comes in: as soon as she sees anything she can acknowledge as the child calming himself down, she thanks him in detail for resetting, deeply connecting around that increment of success. Now all three stands are in collaboration. You can see how this would require the ability to avoid becoming emotionally reactive in response to the child's tantrum.

Over time, as Mom employs these Stands across the board, the child makes the connection: I get the gift of Mom when I calm myself down, even a little bit. I get the gift of Mom when I follow the rules. I get the gift of Mom when I stop breaking rules, and I *don't* get her when I do break rules.

Taking a note from *Scream-Free Parenting*, the First Stand is about refusing to "scream" in response to rules being broken or boundaries pushed. It is about refusing to yell, nag, cajole, lecture, accuse, warn, gently remind, or otherwise focus on what the child isn't doing right or is doing wrong.

Resetting is about being scream-free; about having proper accountability in any interaction with your child. It is about saying to yourself: My kid is not making me feel this way. My kid's choice in this moment is a trigger for me feeling this way. I need to take care of my experience before taking care of the child. It is about stepping out of reaction mode and into either positivity (Stand 2) or clarity (Stand 3).

| MELANIE |

One night in the very early learning stages of NHA, our family was on its way home from dinner out. As soon as we pulled away from the restaurant, the girls started fighting in the back seat. At the same time, Joel got a work phone call on Bluetooth. He started to wave his hand to the back, hoping that his hand would emit magic pixie dust that would stop the girls from fighting. At that point, I had not even begun to master the self-reset. I could consistently reset when I wasn't activated, but when I was, my body went through this weird stage of just kind of...*freezing up*. I ultimately learned to appreciate this, because I realized that doing nothing is better than doing the wrong (reactive) thing.

So, there I was, in the car, with Joel on an anxiety-filled work call, and my girls were going at it in the back seat with seemingly no regard for anyone. I was frozen. Joel looked at me pleadingly, but I had nothing. We drove the whole way home like this. When he hung the phone up, he came in the house and said, "Let's have a family meeting." I was still frozen quiet, but sat down on the couch with the girls to listen to Joel's well-meaning lecture on respect. I watched the girls not listen. I watched my then six-year-old start to do gymnastics on the couch: legs in the air, hands on the floor. Once he'd finished, Joel looked at me. "Well," he said, "do you have anything? Anything you can add?"

I looked at the girls. I felt nothing but a tingle of light…and then, like someone had just replaced my battery pack, it came to me.

"How did you *do* that?!" I yelled.

The girls and Joel stared at me.

"How did you fight the *whole* way home and never make a sound?! That was utterly *brilliant*. I have never seen anyone fight and hit and never make a peep!"

My youngest raised her hand as though she were in school.

"Yes?" Joel and I asked her at the same time.

"It was my fault," she said. "I'm sorry. I shouldn't have hit you."

"It's okay. I love you," Her sister answered.

These girls had never taken responsibility so fast, without prompting. In that moment, where they didn't feel shamed or responsible for taking care of my feelings, they could take care of their own feelings and clean it up the way they felt was best. It was beautiful. That moment will always stand out to me as the first time I truly understood NHA and its power.

THE SELF-RESET, IN REAL LIFE

Resetting is rarely picture-perfect and clean. It can require multiple attempts. The ability to reset ourselves quickly and cleanly in one shot takes time to cultivate. As you begin, allow it to be messy, and try to maintain a sense of curiosity and humor about the process. Always keep

A Brain Science-Based Argument for Positivity

An article by psychology/artificial intelligence student Steven Parton, "The Science of Happiness: Why complaining is literally killing you," went viral on the Web in late 2015.[2] It offers some brain-science-based arguments for accentuating the positive:

Synapses that fire together, wire together.

At the level of neurotransmitters and neurons, the transmission of information across synapses (the miniscule gap between the ends of two neurons) causes those synapses to shrink. In other words, sending information along a specific neural pathway "tightens" that pathway so that transmission happens more quickly the next time. "Your thoughts reshape your brain," Parton writes, and "your brain is always doing this, consistently shifting and morphing with every thought."

[2] http://www.curiousapes.com/the-science-of-happiness-why-complaining-is-literally-killing-you/

in mind that this approach begins with noticing and managing your own energy. This process always takes time and will probably take you through multiple layers of awareness as you hone your skills.

To begin, notice where you are creating connection around what you don't want, through yelling, manipulating, hurrying, scolding, threatening, moralizing, lecturing, teaching, barking, acting like a victim, or expressing self-righteous indignation. Make a conscious choice to *not beat yourself up over any of the above responses* or any that didn't make this list! Absolutely No: refuse to energize the negative in yourself.

Most of us who walk this path are reversing a lifetime pattern of reacting dramatically to problems. Develop the ability to forgive yourself, often, and quickly, any time you slip up. Sometimes, in a moment of chaos, where you feel yourself going down the rabbit-hole of negativity and don't know what to do, the best thing to do is get very quiet. Create space for a reset and it will happen – because it's the natural order of things for calm and balance to be restored.

LINDSEY

Resetting myself in emotionally reactive moments requires a certain amount of strategy and forethought. To get out of an entrenched pattern of reactivity, I must actively decide that a calmer approach and a better outcome with my child is more important than maintaining the comforting familiarity of my historical responses. When I am in a reactive moment, I can call upon certain motivating thoughts or ideas to calm myself down. I use these higher intentions as leverage to cut through the intense survival instinct that leads to habitual reactions. Some of my own key leverage points are:

1. My desire to model the behavior I want to encourage in my kids.
2. The knowledge that if I am reactive, my kids' attention will be on my behavior rather than their own (mis)behavior.
3. My past experiences: when I've managed to remain calm, the resulting interactions with my children are more interesting, surprising and transformative than when I lose my cool.

    Currently, (3) is probably my biggest motivator. When I'm struggling to remain calm, it is powerful if I can remember that if I revert to reactivity, I set myself up for the same old fights and patterns. If I can stay present and connected, something new, creative, and unexpected can take place.

The pattern of your synapses creates your default personality.

By repeating thought patterns, you create an advantage for certain aspects of your personality that might seem innate but are the result of a groove dug ever-deeper through specific patterns of thought.

Your choices in this regard impact the structure and function of the brains of people around you.

Others' complaining and negativity impact your thoughts and feelings in a very real way. We all have "mirror neurons" in our brains that are designed to pick up on and mirror the attitudes and emotions of other people. This is empathy; it's natural, and its original purposes in human survival probably had to do with the ability to think, work and feel as part of a collective in our tribes. Unfortunately, it can also serve to drag people down into others' negativity and complaining mindsets. And remember, neurons that fire together, wire together: so, other people's complaints make *your* brain better at going negative. Being exposed to others' negativity will also activate stress hormones in your body (more on this in Chapter Three). When you bring your negativity to the table, it impacts others in that same way.

The flip side: hanging around with people who are positive and loving will make you more positive and loving, too; and your influence, in turn, will do the same for others.

Parton draws his article to a rousing conclusion: *...regardless of what [life] brings your way, your choice is simple: Love or Fear. And yes, I understand it's hard to find happiness on those nights when you feel like you're all alone in the world, when a loved one passes, when you fail that test or get fired from that job; but when these moments come, you do not have to...give them constant negative attention and allow them to reshape your brain to the point that you become a bitter, jaded, cynical old curmudgeon that no longer notices that the very fact that they're alive means they get to play blissfully in this cosmic playground.*

The NHA is built to support parents in making "time-in" – that time when no rules are being broken and all is well – much more exciting than time-out. When created with intention and skill, time-in is an open opportunity to propel success, inner wealth, and greatness. This is achieved through the attitudes and techniques of Stand 2.

STAND 2: ABSOLUTELY YES!

Let's look at ways to relentlessly energize positivity – including any area in which negativity is not being expressed in this moment.

When we first caught on to this notion of recognizing a child for *not* breaking the rules or for doing the smallest things right, we hit the wall. It felt awkward and ran counter to most of our intuitions about parenting.

Are you kidding me? Don't tackle the problem?

Don't jump in when struggle is happening?

Don't race to help solve a sibling issue or help a child who is having a meltdown?

What are we supposed to do instead?

This is where Stand 2 comes in. **Stand 2 – "absolutely YES!" – is about transferring all the energy once put behind correcting and fixing problems into finding right choices, positive expressions, and examples of the child living their greatness.** These are the moments when profound teaching can take place: when things are going the way we want them to go. The trick is to channel our desire to teach and inspire into moments when we can 'accuse' the child of being and living the very solution we were wanting in the first place. It is about learning to see what's going well at both large and small scales; about cultivating genuine gratitude for these expressions; and about developing language for sharing what we see with the child.

Gratefulness is the conduit to being full of greatness. This approach supports parents in developing and using their own unique language to express the undercurrent of greatness that's always there to draw upon.

TECHNIQUES TO SUPPORT
THE SECOND STAND

Each of these techniques builds on the one before it. Implement them one at a time. Take a few days to practice the first before adding the second, and so on. Once you've moved through all of them individually, you'll find yourself seamlessly combining them. You will have developed a new way of talking to your child about what's going well.

Active Recognition. Watch the child carefully, and then describe to the child what you see or otherwise sense. Withhold any judgment; just reflect what you are seeing in the present moment. Begin with lead-ins like "I see…" "I hear…" "I notice…" "I'm sensing…" or even "Sounds like…" or "Seems to me like…"

"I see you playing quietly with your toys."

"I hear you singing along with your music!"

"I notice you getting up from the couch and walking toward your room."

Active Recognitions are also useful for capturing a child in a moment of feeling strong emotions. Having an adult notice their emotional state helps develop the child's emotional intelligence.

"I sense you're feeling angry right now."

"You seem very excited. Your smile is lighting up the whole room!"

Active Recognitions let your child know that they are truly *seen* in moments where nothing is going wrong. They are following the rules, and they are being appreciated. Combined, the absence of value judgments plus irrefutable, inarguable evidence of what is happening in the moment make these statements both incontrovertible and easy to take in. Active Recognition moves past the resistance of the child who might probably resist more direct positive statements.

Active Recognitions are least likely to bring up resistance from the child, as they don't rely on interpretations that might conflict with the child's self-perception. A child who is used to being recognized mostly for negativity, or one who is especially self-critical, may resist even these simple, validating recognitions – but that is truly rare. These recognitions seem to reliably go under the radar while still conveying a sense of success.

Even if the child seems resistant, don't back off; this means that you are having an impact! If the child reacts angrily or disrespectfully, remember that you are trying to shift an entrenched dynamic where the child gets more of YOU for being "bad." Instead, stand your ground: dig into more statements about what you recognize as successful in the moment. For example: "I can tell you don't like what I said. By the look on your face, I can tell you want me to go away, and that you think what I said was weird. It was weird for me too…but I've decided to see you in a more positive way and appreciate you more, so hopefully, I'll get used to it. Maybe you will too. In the meantime, thanks for not yelling."

Experiential Recognition. An Experiential Recognition is an Active Recognition plus a statement of appreciation regarding how the child's actions reveal their *qualities of greatness* – the great aspects that are integral and intrinsic to who they are. What do you see, hear, or otherwise experience the child doing? What do you appreciate about what this shows about who this child is?

The basic structure of an Experiential Recognition is:

"I see/hear/notice/sense you *[action/emotion]*…this shows me that you *[quality of greatness]…[statement of appreciation/acknowledgement]*. For example: "I see you brushing your teeth before heading to school… this shows me that you care about the health of your teeth and about having fresh breath…that you have the greatness of self-care and consideration for others. I'm really appreciating that quality in you."

| MELANIE |

One day I waited in my car in the line to pick up my daughter from school. She called me, asking if she could go with her friends to a nearby restaurant for a little while. I was annoyed because I was already there, and told her no. She pleaded for a few minutes; I held firm, and when she got in the car, she smiled hello and was quiet. I told her how proud I was of her for taking a disappointment well and maturely. I talked about how impressed I was by her self-control. When I brought it up again at dinner, she said, "I was really angry at you," and I was able to further energize how much her admission of anger further showed how much self-control she had used. She didn't say anything to that.

Then, at bedtime, I mentioned it one more time. She said, "Please stop it, Mom, I hate when you make a big deal over things like this." I turned to her and said, "I know you hate it when I do this. But I know we both agree that it is better than me making a big deal over things gone wrong. You're going to have to find a way to get comfortable with it." She smiled, turned over, and went to sleep. We both felt good! Amazing how easy it would have been to let this small success slide right by, and how truly good it feels to celebrate these moments. I know I am teaching her, in an experiential way, how self-control looks and feels. It is so important for my own process as well…it reminds me to always be looking for and creating positive experiences with my children.

Attempts to teach positive values when they are perceived to be lacking enhance the child's impression that they get more of YOU when things are going wrong. A child who is in the throes of a negative reaction or acting out is not receptive to learning or self-reflection; they may even be in a state of fight-or-flight (more on this in the next chapter), which limits their capacity to absorb information or make meaningful changes in their behavior. Capturing and describing in detail a moment where the child is being honest, respectful, or responsible, even in a small way, has more positive impact.

"I see you playing quietly with your toys. You are directing yourself in a way that keeps you busy and happy, and you're being considerate of me and my need to finish paying the bills."

"I hear you singing along with your music! I love how expressive you are."

"I notice you're getting up from the couch and walking toward your room. Looks like you're thinking about the next thing you need to get done before we leave for school. Great forethought and responsibility."

"I sense you're feeling angry right now. You're staying pretty calm and that takes a lot of self-control when you're angry."

"You seem very excited. Your smile is lighting up the whole room! I love how much joy you bring just by showing up and expressing yourself."

To us, at first, this felt so incredibly hard. It felt false, even foolish. It is so easy to articulate what is going wrong, but we could barely string together three words of acknowledgment until we'd practiced for about three months. Be gentle with yourself; hold a playful and self-forgiving attitude as you experiment with these recognitions.

JENNIFER[3]

One day during second grade, my son Kieran was feeling self-conscious about arriving late to school after a doctor's appointment. I calmly, firmly walked with him through the parking lot at school. It was VERY slow. We took one step every five seconds, but every time Kieran moved forward, I acknowledged the progress. I did a lot of resetting of my own impatience so I could continue to give him this positive feedback. When we finally made it through the front gate, Kieran became overwhelmed at the thought of entering the classroom, interrupting whatever was happening and drawing unwanted attention to himself. So, once again, I reset my own need for this to end quickly. I led him into the

---

[3] In this story, names and relevant details have been changed to protect the privacy of those who shared it with us.

school office so he could gather himself while I checked in with his teachers about a good transition time. I came back to the office, acknowledged that he had calmed himself down and then explained the morning's schedule to him. My sweet, brave boy dried his tears and grabbed his backpack to head to class. As he walked away, I told him he was a superhero and that he had just leapt over Empire State Building-sized feelings!

Proactive Recognition. Children tend to have an adversarial relationship with the rules. This isn't surprising, considering that they are used to only hearing about rules when they are being broken. This technique gives adults words with which to celebrate children when they are not breaking the rules. It requires that we get clear about what the rules are – where the line is drawn – and that we commit to reinforcing the child when he is on the side of rules being followed.

REIMAGINING YOUR HOUSE RULES

The first step to building Proactive Recognitions is taking a fresh look at the rules you wish to be followed. More specifically, it entails stating your rules beginning with the word "no": *No hitting. No cursing. No lying. No leaving a mess in the kitchen. No teasing your siblings. No refusing to do homework.* This runs contrary to much modern parenting wisdom, which holds that rules should be stated as positives, as things to aspire to: *Be responsible. Be kind to others. Keep your hands to yourself.*

Stating rules in this way, in the positive, makes absolute clarity around them difficult. Imagine a basketball court where the sideline is drawn not in a straight clear line, but where it's wiggly, faint, and wavy. That's what 'positive' rules are like to the child. To the intense child, they are an invitation to push limits to try to determine where exactly the line is.

Old rule: Be respectful.

New rules: No interrupting adults when they are speaking. No cursing. No smartphone use at the table. No teasing. No cruel language.

Old rule: Keep your hands to yourself.

New rules: No hitting. No kicking. No poking. No tickling without the ticklee's consent. No pushing. No throwing things at people.

Take a few minutes to re-imagine your house rules along these lines. You may find that "be respectful" breaks down into a lot of rules starting with "no." That's all right – having lots of rules is better. More rules mean more positives to recognize, since most of them *aren't* being broken at any given time.

Also, when children recognize that the consequence for a broken rule is, most of the time, a simple reset and new opportunity to *follow* that same rule, their fear of breaking rules will shift to recognition that they can reset and recover. As your child catches on to this, it will transform their relationship to rules.

Do you need to write your new rules out or post them? You can if you want to – particularly if it helps you, as the adult, to gain clarity – but it is almost never necessary for your child. If you are clear about the rules, your child already knows what they are, no matter how you phrase them. Do you need to review them with your children? Won't hurt, but probably is not necessary. You can introduce them via skillful Proactive Recognitions and reinforce them via third-stand resets.

Use Proactive Recognitions to institute new rules on the fly. Let's say a child throws a ball inside the house. Give a reset, and then, as soon as they aren't throwing the ball, say, "Thanks for resetting. I see you are now following the rule about not throwing balls in the house. That shows respect for our belongings." If they say, "I didn't know that was a rule," you can shrug and say, "It wasn't, until now! Thanks again for following it. You're being considerate. You're not creating a risk of breaking the glass in the framed photos on the table. Also, you're making sure my body is safe from being hit by the ball inside the house."

The most essential ingredient is cultivating your own ability to have a toll taker/baby steps/miracles from molecules attitude about rules not broken.

Most of the time, even the most challenging child is not breaking any rules, and this creates vast new territory for recognition.

Here's the formula: Proactive Recognition = Appreciation of rule not broken + Experiential Recognition.

"Thanks for following our rule about no smartphone use at the table. I see you left your phone in your bag instead of taking it out. That shows me your thoughtfulness and that you appreciate how important it is for us to connect face to face. I feel respected and valued."

You can say this *even if you see your child about to break the rule.* You can notice the child reaching into their bag for their phone, and seize the moment where they are still following the rule...even if you both sense they are about to break it! The truth of the moment is that they haven't, and that's what can be honestly expressed.

"I notice you are following our rule about no hitting. I see your brother's getting on your nerves, and you're really keeping your cool."

"You didn't break our rule about arguing with adults. Even though I can see you so want to argue with me, you're holding back. That's great emotional regulation."

LINDSEY

> My daughter saved her money and bought a Kindle Fire. Since the device had Internet access, her use was subject to our house rule of no Internet in her bedroom. One evening, she found it too tempting, and we discovered that she had switched from reading her book to surfing the Web. I acknowledged that she broke a rule and that was a bummer, but I admired and appreciated that she didn't try to pretend that she wasn't on the Internet when we caught her. This showed her integrity and honesty. She broke down in tears, saying she was worried that I wouldn't trust her anymore. I told her that she just made a mistake, but that she had given me excellent evidence that she is a trustworthy person by coming clean about having broken the rule.

An important point: Once a rule is broken – once the line has been crossed – the time for Proactive Recognition (or any other kind of recognition) is past. It's time to give an un-energized reset to the child. Positive recognitions can be given within seconds of the reset; wait until the rule is no longer being violated.

Creative Recognition. This final technique provides parents with a way to appreciate a child for complying with a request. It is a useful tool for getting started with positivity when it feels hard to find things to acknowledge. The parent makes a clear request (not a question, but a statement) with which the child is likely to have trouble *not* complying.

A few examples:

- The child is putting toothpaste on her toothbrush. "I need you to brush your teeth," the parent might say, and then jump right into appreciations. "Thanks for getting right on that. Your self-care habits are terrific. That's going to serve you well over the years, taking such good care of your teeth."

- The child is in the car, starting to close the door. "Close the door," the parent might say, and unless they literally stop mid-close, they can't help but comply. "You did that really fast! Reflexes like a cat." As they put on their seatbelt, wondering if the parent has lost her mind: "Now please put on your seatbelt." Click. "You're way ahead of me today! Love that you're so on top of staying safe in the car." And so on.

- Notice that the requests are made in the imperative. No "Will you please…" or anything else that implies a choice. Also, notice that the child gets full credit for complying with the request, even if it would require actively reversing their actions to avoid compliance.

| LINDSEY |

My daughter decided she wanted to quit her Friday afternoon ballet class. I told her she needed to go to one last class for the month I had paid for, and then I would unregister her. She tried everything to get me to change my mind: reasoning with me, crying, yelling, begging, insulting, manipulating, and even sinking to the floor in despair.

The more she reacted/acted out, the more my instincts told me to calmly and without negativity insist on the boundary I had chosen and see this through. I gave her positive reflections wherever I could: for not escalating further, for being real about what she was feeling, even for her endurance in trying to get her way! I stuck to my guns through the firestorm of her reactions and accusations. I finally told her that I needed her to get into her dance clothes and meet me at the car, and we'd be as late as she decided, depending on how fast she could get ready. I sat in the car and waited and when she appeared in her leotard and tights and got in the car, I acknowledged the strength it took to make that choice, given how upset she was about my decision.

On the 15-minute drive to the studio, she went back through the cycle of asking, pleading, begging, and crying, and then moved on to insulting me ("You're just a DANCE MOM who cares more about me going to class than you care about ME!"). My heart never closed. I never lost my cool. I mostly kept quiet and refused to energize the conversation while she ranted. When we arrived at the class six minutes late – which she said was my fault – she told me that I was a horrible person and that she hated me. Then, she got out, slammed the car door, and ran into class.

My kids have instinctively picked up on my fears about losing relationship and connection with them. Since I began using the NHA, my daughter has doubled down to see if she can get her favorite toy to dance to that tune. I don't think she had ever actually said she hated me before. I had to sit with that momentary feeling of rejection while she stormed away. Instead of yelling or lecturing at her, I sat with my feelings and sensations until they subsided. When she got in the car at the end of the class an hour later, my daughter was calm and pleasant to be with. I took the opportunity to acknowledge her for the strength, maturity and self-control it had taken to move forward and participate in the ballet class when she had wanted so desperately to avoid it.

Something in her attempted refusal to go to this class struck me as a test that I needed to pass. I needed to stay calm and strong in my decision, even when the underlying outcome (going to the dance class or not) didn't amount to a particularly important issue. She was trying every tool in her toolbox to inspire my reactivity, and it felt important that I calmly demonstrate that none of them would work.

FROM 'FAKING 'TIL YOU MAKE IT' TO KEEPING IT REAL

When you are first learning the approach, you may find yourself "faking 'til you make it" when it comes to finding positives and acknowledging them. Self-resetting requires practice and patience, and there may be many occasions where you give what feels like a truly far-fetched positive acknowledgement through gritted teeth – when doing so is the last thing you want to do, and where gratitude feels light-years away. You'll know you aren't reset, and you'll do your best to hold on to Stands One and Two even when you're not feeling it. Even doing the Approach in this white-knuckle way will probably yield dramatic shifts. If you don't let the child in on your angst, it will make a difference.

The growing edge, however, is to move determinedly toward giving greater Stand 2 acknowledgements authentically, when you are connected to the child and when *you* are fully reset; taking any energy that is propelling you toward lectures, punishments, or other energies toward negativity and channeling it into a bigger, better Second Stand appreciations and recognitions of cleaner, clearer rules *now not broken*.

In a TED talk that has been viewed over 12 million times, social science researcher Amy Cuddy talks about her research on body posture, brain chemistry, and outcomes in people's lives. She shares her findings that adopting a so-called "power pose" – where the body is expansive and open – for only two minutes creates significant changes In Cuddy's research, when subjects adopted a power pose (chest lifted, head high, arms akimbo or raised), testosterone – the hormone of dominance and leadership – rose; when subjects adopted low-power poses (constricted, arms folded, making the body smaller, putting a hand to one's own neck or face), testosterone fell. Levels of the stress hormone cortisol fell in the power-pose subjects and rose in the low-power pose subjects.

Cuddy shares that some people who hear about this research are afraid that of eventually being revealed as impostors, making their way into places they don't belong by adopting a fake body posture designed to help them feel more powerful than they are. She points out that over time, as we make small adjustments in body posture to help us be more powerful in our lives, we become that more powerful person we have been embodying. Her take-home message: "Don't just fake it till you make it – fake it till you BECOME it."

Steadily, relentlessly practice that skillset of stopping, resetting, and consciously channeling the energy and intensity of your own resistance and any related frustrations into Second Stand acknowledgments. It is all energy that is available to be transformed. When you are in a triggered moment and feel as though you might explode, *grab onto that energy with all your might and turn it in a different direction.* Hold on to this practice when you are faced with difficult emotions and sensations that make you want to react; you will discover a new capacity to act according to your higher intentions as those feelings move through you, and eventually you will learn to channel that energy into enhanced recognitions and clarity. As you pretend to be reset and squawk out a forced acknowledgement; as you maintain the body posture of a person who is NOT available for negativity – trust that you are changing your nervous system, one reset at a time. This practice can complement any deeper therapeutic or mindfulness work you are doing to heal past traumas or better cope with challenging situations. Some strong feelings can be almost overwhelming and make one want to push them away. Using this energy is a great way of being both honest with yourself (that yes, that emotions are there, and they are powerful) and putting that very same energy toward making you more strong, determined, purposeful, and skillful.

As you fumble your way through the techniques and Stands, appreciate yourself for your own effort and commitment. As you gain mastery with weaving techniques together and finding ways to reset yourself, energize yourself for every movement toward authentic appreciation and greater levels of resetting yourself. More will be said about this self-energizing in the chapter on Nurtured Heart Appreciative Coaching (Chapter Eight).

BEFORE YOU MOVE INTO STAND 3

- **Take time – a few days to a few weeks – to work Stands One and Two.** Strive to maintain your new attunement and commitment to not giving the gifts of your energy, connection, and relationship to negativity. Create a consistently alluring time-in before adding your new approach to time-out.
- **During that time, maintain the same system of consequences for broken rules that you have had up until now,** but suck as much of the energy and connection out of those consequences as possible.
- **Work with a specific and growing awareness on recognizing where your own reactivity comes up** and notice how this can interfere with your ability to follow Stands One and Two.

THE THIRD STAND: ABSOLUTELY CLEAR!

This stand involves enforcing clear limits and consequences with a minimum of energetic charge. It means *always* providing a true "consequence" when a rule is broken. Hopefully, your child has witnessed you resetting yourself by now. If not, let them know that you have begun this practice, and how much it has helped you. Let them know that from now on, you'll be using a form of this reset as a reminder to them to follow the rules if they forget to do so; and that you'll be doing this instead of administering lectures, yelling, and handing out punishments and warnings.

A **Stand 3 reset is a pause in adult engagement with a child in immediate response to the child breaking a rule.** It can last anywhere from a few seconds to a couple of minutes. The key is to give the reset, and then to be on the lookout for the next moment where the rule is not being broken. As soon as that moment is perceived, you acknowledge the child for resetting to a place where they are now following the rule. It is a pause and an invitation to begin again, just like the end of the video game or the time-out in the sporting event. *To the child, the reset is felt as a consequence – even if it doesn't seem that way based on the child's response or the adult's sense of how a consequence is supposed to land.*

The simple format is this: "[Child's name], reset." The energetic subtext is not "Gotcha!" or "How dare you?!" but "Oops! Broke a rule. Time to pause and remember yourself." Resist the temptation to explain which rule was broken – at least, not until you can do it in the context of the rule being followed, through Proactive Recognition.

As soon as the truth of the moment comes back around to some form of success, end the reset. "Thanks for resetting. I appreciate now that you aren't [whatever the broken rule is]." Howard compares this with pulling the plug on the energy between you and the child in response to rule-breaking, then purposefully plugging it in again to create a new surge of positive connection as the rule is no longer broken or the child's energy shifts in a direction away from the rule-breaking behavior.

─── **LINDSEY** ────────────────────────────────

Our daughter brought her smartphone in her room overnight, which is against our house rules. When David and I reset her the next morning, she was angry and defensive and tried to paint us as overprotective and unreasonable. We stayed calm and matter-of-fact. It was hard for me – I was triggered by her accusations and felt alienated from her, but I knew I couldn't act out at her in response to those feelings, because I would then end up energizing the exact thing I didn't want.

She stormed off and I felt horrible, but 10 minutes later she wanted me to sit with her while she did her homework and wanted me to read to her at bedtime. The next day she made me a card that said, "I love you." In her way, she was thanking me for giving her a clear boundary along with a sense of being calmly and capably parented. Children appreciate the clarity of Stand 3, even if they don't immediately show that appreciation when caught breaking a rule.

It's up to you to decide when the reset ends. Until then, the child misses out on time-in – that is, a fun and rewarding connection with her favorite toy (you). If you've created a sufficient level of nourishment in time-in, even a few seconds of missing out feels like a true consequence to the child.

When the child is in reset, avoid lectures, warnings, sympathies, coaching, or expressions of emotion. Reset yourself when you have the urge to dive into relationship around bad behavior. **Actively channel the energy of big emotions into positive recognitions following the reset.** Anything that delivers connected relationship during the reset will feed the child's impression that you're available in response to negativity.

It may take some time for the child to recognize that the new status quo is not going to change. Continue to reset yourself (Stand 1), pour on the positives (Stand 2), and be clear about resetting every instance of a broken rule (Stand 3). These three parts of the approach lock together and balance one another.

| LINDSEY |

Our teenaged daughter was reticent to participate in family activities and togetherness over the holidays. Instead, she would retreat to another room to text her friends or go on Instagram. When we asked her why, she gave us a variety of excuses: she didn't like the game we were playing; she wasn't interested in the movie we were watching; she was too tired; or none of the cousins were her age. We were willing to write some of this off as normal teenage aloofness, but we also insisted that she had to be with us and participate on a semi-regular basis, whether she wanted to or not. The problem is that I was constantly nagging her and she seemed to retreat more and more. We were in a cycle of low-grade negativity that wasn't getting us anywhere and certainly didn't make time with me seem appealing to her.

At one point, she emerged from her room, passing my husband and I while we were in the kitchen. We didn't know whether her plan was to join the group or whether she had chosen to come out because she needed something, but my husband said to her, "I know how good it feels to be on social media and texting your friends in privacy. That's an understandable thing to want. And now you're choosing to come out and be present and connected with your family during the holiday. I can see you trusting yourself to know when to find time to connect with your friends too. It's nice to see you!" For the next couple of days, our daughter joined in meals and other group activities without being asked, or with only minor encouragement.

Your goal is not to make the child fear breaking rules; this consequence is the opposite of scary. It is to make rule-breaking boring while creating drama and excitement around rules being followed. With the Nurtured Heart Approach, the drama and excitement come from the stirring of the soul through lighting up the runway of goodness and greatness for the child. Remember the energetics of video games and favorite toys: the most effective way to bring a child to change a problematic behavior is to (1) make sure the results of that behavior are as uninteresting as possible, while (2) creating growing interest in the vastly positive realm of non-problematic behaviors.

Please trust that for almost all normal rule violations, the simple reset alone is the most powerful path to change. More extreme infractions may seem to call for restoration, repair, or longer-term restrictions, but keep in mind that in adding extras onto the simple reset – removing electronics, for example, or grounding, or giving extra chores – you risk giving the child the perception that they get more relationship in response to their negative choice.

If you do choose to add to the simple reset at this point, keep conversations around it as un-energized and concise as possible. Give appreciation for every aspect of restoration or repair as it is completed. If you choose to ground the child for a few days, for example, appreciate every possible aspect of her accepting the consequence gracefully. Again, anything other than the simplicity of the reset is almost always unnecessary.

MELANIE

A way I leak negativity sometimes is in what Glasser would call the CSI – Crime Scene Investigation. I expend energy and spend time mulling over *why* my child is acting out. *What's going on with her? What's happening that she needs the stimulation of a fight? Is she trying to connect with her feelings? Does she need some kind of release or 'explosion' because her emotions are pent-up? Is she bored and doesn't know what else to do but create some drama?*

All these are possibilities, and in the end, the "why" doesn't matter. Delving into the "why" means staying in the past. NHA at its cleanest is always about staying in the present moment and finding what's right within it; about releasing stories about why something might have happened, releasing fears that it might happen in the next moment, and identifying and talking about the gifts of the present moment.

NOTCHING IT UP

Howard tells a story about a family that approached him for direct NHA coaching after he had shifted to leading trainings and workshops and no longer taking private clients. They told him that they were doing the approach the best they could and that it wasn't working.

"Do this approach for the next two weeks *as though your life depended on it,*" he told them. "If, after those two weeks, you still want my help, I'll give it to you." At the end of those two weeks, the parents had worked the approach to the level that was required on their own.

This working of the approach is called *notching it up.* Notching it up means taking the intensity and clarity of the approach to the level at which it succeeds. It means responding to a child's difficult behaviors with ever-stronger adherence to the Stands of the approach. No matter the opposition or resistance, the notching-up process is always the same, varying only in the energetic push required to meet the latest challenge.

Notching up Stand 1: More cleanly refuse to give energy to negativity.

Notching up Stand 2: Give more positive acknowledgments. Give them with greater energy and commitment. Boost the ways in which you connect those acknowledgements to greatness. Get more "squeaky-clean" (Howard's term) around giving recognitions for all rules not being broken.

Notching up Stand 3: Get even more clear about the rules and about resetting the child when a rule is broken.

When the approach isn't working, or when the child is resisting or escalating in response to the approach, the solution is always to *notch up* the Three Stands. In the *Transforming the Intense Child Workbook,*

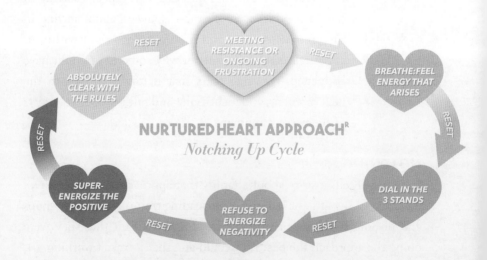

notching it up is depicted as a cycle. Each step leads through a reset and into a new level of positivity and helps guide you in moving energy from negativity into supporting the Three Stands at progressively greater levels.

| HOWIE |

I was in a bad traffic accident recently. A truck ran a red light and took off the front of my car. It looked as though the truck was going to come right through me; miraculously, it ended up only damaging the vehicles. Both drivers were OK.

As I sat there in the aftermath before shock set in, I felt total lucidity and clarity. Running through my mind was a singular thought, which felt directed at the other driver: *Never. Run. A. Red. Light. Again.* And when the other driver came over while the EMTs were checking me out, that's exactly what I said: "Don't you EVER do that again." He was enormously apologetic.

I had said exactly what I needed to say and nothing more. It was clear. I was feeling some pretty strong emotions, but I was able to reset them cleanly and express them succinctly and powerfully. This is the outcome of many years of consistent practice in resetting myself. I've gotten to the point where I can be supercharged with emotion and move that energy into truthful AND heart-based communication.

This is Nurtured Heart-style limit-setting: It started with my own deep reset (Stand 1), where I took the energy of what was absolutely true in the moment and directed it and renewed it. I'm not going to give my energy to negativity, but I'm going to feel everything that wants to be felt. I am going to feel the truth of my own emotional state whether I am worried, fearful, angry, enraged, ecstatic, playful, or in whatever other emotional state that is real for me in the moment. Having done this completely, I can mindfully take advantage of any energy and use it as fuel for growing greatness. This enables me to express what is true for me without losing that clarity.

One caveat: Expressing your deepest truth to a child who believes, in the moment, that they get more from life through negativity can backfire. The way I responded to the driver who took off the front of my car would not be appropriate with a child who is actively looking for a way to get my goat. When working to shift lifelong patterns of energy for negativity, too much transparency around challenging emotions will fuel the fire of negativity. The truth-telling becomes part of your own internal, Stand 1 reset, and not a part of your outward expression to the child.

If I am trying to be clear with somebody and I haven't achieved Stand 1, I might still be edgy from negativity. In those cases, I always get stunningly powerful feedback from the universe: the conversation does not go well. If I had not reset my rage at the driver for running the red light, I might have leaked some strong negativity and been met by reactivity. What I did, instead, was drink in that wave of energy and convert it to honest clarity. I gave my energy to the clear message.

Nurtured Heart is a *truth-based approach*. If a child is not acting out, we tell the truth. If they are being respectful, we are not going to overlook that; we are going to be in the truth of those moments. If the child looks like they *may* act out but haven't, we reflect the positive truth that they are *not* acting out in this moment. If they do act out, they get a reset – the truth-based result of that choice.

The energy of truth is love. Following the energy of truth is a very loving way to live one's life.

CHAPTER THREE

EMOTIONAL FLOODING:
when Resetting is Hard

If you feel safe and loved, your brain becomes specialized in exploration, play, and cooperation. If you are frightened and unwanted, it specializes in managing feelings of fear and abandonment.

- Bessel Van der Kolk, M.D., *The Body Keeps the Score: Brain, Mind, and Body in the Healing of Trauma*. Penguin Books, 2014: p. 56.

A major premise of this book, and of the Nurtured Heart Approach in general, is that parenting works best and is easiest and simplest when parents can remain calm when things get challenging. Really, *all* our relationships are likely to be healthier and happier when we can regulate our emotions in trying times.

Some of the ways we respond to stressful situations is constitutional. As parents, we know that some human beings arrive in the world calmer or more reactive than others. We can see these traits in our children in their earliest weeks of life. Current thinking in the psychology world suggests, however, that our upbringings powerfully impact our reactions to situations that challenge us – that "nurture" matters as much as (or more than) "nature." The way we are parented has a dramatic impact on the way we respond to others and the way we ultimately parent our own children. Even a sensitive, intense child can become good at not flipping out under stress if their parents set a good example for them and provide emotional education. A naturally calm child can be made reactive if early relationships set the stage for reactivity.

"Default" ways of relating are built within us by the ways we are parented in our earliest months and years, before we develop the ability to express ourselves through language. This encoding can make it difficult to shift such patterns, because they aren't reachable through cognitive reasoning. Default ways of relating to others first develop within the young, pre-verbal self, and they feel automatic, like a part of who we are. They don't operate in terms of higher brain functions linked to language. Therefore, standard talk-based psychotherapy may not be the most effective way to shift these kinds of deeply entrenched reactive patterns – they run on an energetic frequency and don't truck in reason or logic.

The defaults our own parents installed in us are likely the ones installed in them by their own parents when they were very young. Your ability to manage your emotional responses to your child is established, in part, by those old defaults – in combination with other factors like life stresses, your internal makeup, the intensity of your child, your culture's expectations of your child and your parenting, and whatever other social, psychological or biochemical challenges you face on any given day.

Let's not ignore that, as social animals, we are wired to be reactive in certain situations that suggest danger at a non-verbal level. Consider a herd of antelope grazing on the savannah. If one hears a noise and looks up, what does the rest of the herd do? They all snap to attention. If no threat turns out to be present, they go back to their grazing; if a predator is creeping toward the herd, and one antelope sees it first, they move as one creature, darting at top speed to escape being eaten. Humans are not so different. When in a room with others, we subconsciously, instinctively read their energy. If they seem angry or on high alert, our physiology picks up on that. Without conscious awareness, we read others' postures, expressions, and gestures, and this all helps us to determine whether we and our loved ones are safe. Knowing we have this great ability to attune to others, we can bring this knowledge into conscious awareness and recognize where our reactivity jumps up a few notches for this reason.

The antelope, in their natural environment, can go back and forth easily from high alert to calmly grazing. Humans don't seem to be as good at this. For one thing, the dangers that create anxiety or fear for most of us aren't the kind we can run away from. In addition, humans tend to create stories in our heads about the "dangers" we face. We think that things should or shouldn't be happening; we blame others for our perceived jeopardy; and we get stuck in reliving past danger or predicting future danger. For these and many other reasons, we humans don't tend to just shake off the high alert state and return to the present moment.

When we first learned the Nurtured Heart Approach, we recognized how big a difference it made even when we used it clumsily, without feeling it in our hearts and bones. But we came to see that to "notch it up" – to evolve our abilities to use it effectively, and to feel the approach as a way of being – we had to look at what was in the way of our being able to consistently uphold the Stands. We had to take time to identify unconscious patterns that were sabotaging our parenting, and to continually work to become more connected and authentic. The more we dedicated ourselves to this kind of "clearing the runway," the better the Nurtured Heart Approach felt when we stepped back into parenting our children. The more the words coming out of our mouths came to match the energy our kids sensed in us, the more powerful the impact of the Three Stands became.

We weren't alone in recognizing this as a fundamental challenge in using this approach. At trainings and in parent groups we have often heard people – usually, mothers – initially respond to the idea of the self-reset as a great idea in theory, but extremely challenging in practice.

In this chapter and the next one, we'll more deeply examine why resetting can be harder for some than for others. We'll examine the physical reasons for emotional overwhelm and support you in recognizing how old and new patterns of interaction with yourself and others might be lowering your threshold. We'll guide you – based on our own experience and with guidance from Nurtured Heart principles and practices – in learning specific tools for managing your emotions, moment-to-moment.

No matter where you begin, three essential truths apply:

Emotional management is key to good parenting. Every time you lose your cool with your child, you fortify their impression that breaking rules and pushing buttons yield a more interesting response and relationship than expressions of greatness. Every time you *don't* lose your cool and reset yourself instead, you demonstrate this valuable life skill for your child/ren and help them learn to regulate their own emotional reactions.

Emotional management can seem easy when things are going well, but it's in moments where they *aren't* that this skill is most needed. When a child has found your most reactive "buttons" and is pushing them like mad, you are in the most pivotal moment with that child. Building your emotional management resources during calmer times will prepare you to reset in those moments.

Emotional management is a skillset that can (and should) be learned and practiced to prepare for those pivotal moments. Whether you are someone who gets triggered occasionally; someone for whom parenting is a constant emotional minefield; or someone whose reactivity falls somewhere between these extremes – understanding how emotions work, what influences our thresholds for emotional overwhelm, and how to manage emotions will support you in maintaining the First Stand.

| VIOLET[4] |

Henry and I married in 2013 – my second marriage, his first. We each brought a child to the equation. By the time we all moved in together, his son Jon was well over six feet tall, physically mature beyond his 14 years.

---

[4] In this story, names and relevant details have been changed to protect the privacy of those who shared it with us.

His mother had been challenged with a mental health diagnosis and his father had endured abuse during his own difficult childhood. Soon after we became a family, things started to go wrong. Jon was chronically truant; refused to do schoolwork; stole money from family members; used and sold prescription and illicit drugs; sneaked out almost nightly; and was addicted to his smartphone and online gaming. As the parents tried to rein him in, there were violent outbursts in the home. He lied compulsively, was anxious and depressed, and self-harmed.

At first, I believed that with the Nurtured Heart Approach, this toxic dynamic could be transformed. Jon had a lot of magnificent qualities worth energizing. He was bright, charming, and funny, a natural leader and a devoted friend. He could be sweetly vulnerable and authentic. We had wonderful talks. But by July of 2015, Jon had become too difficult to control at home and a clear risk to himself and others, and we sent him to a therapeutic boarding school thousands of miles away, where he was able to course-correct in a way we could not facilitate at home.

Once Jon left, I had to face the fact that I had failed miserably with the approach I believed in so strongly. I had allowed my ongoing and obvious dismay at his choices to take over my house, my brain, and my partner relationship. Every day, I had felt tense from first thing in the morning to bedtime, waiting for the next piece of bad news from his teacher or his dad.

I had tried to hold on to my Stands, but my emotions kept overwhelming my efforts. Even when I could maintain the first Stand – pretending, through gritted teeth, that the latest issue didn't bother me, and trying to maintain clear rules and limits – I felt like a failure. The tools were there for me; I knew they would work, even if in the tiniest increments. Why couldn't I get myself to use them? They seemed locked away, beyond my reach. I could maintain my usual positivity with my own child, but this made things worse with Jon.

When handed a situation that truly challenged me, I had reverted to reactivity, lecturing, yelling, negative expectations and catastrophic thinking. For months, I had walked around stressed, steeped in negativity, resistant to connection, and ready to blow. Never for a moment did I doubt that the NHA was the only way through, even as I faced how far I'd swung away from my intentions as a parent.

Violet's situation had sent her into a perpetually emotionally flooded state. In that place, she couldn't use the approach that she knew would afford the best chance of solving the issues she faced with her son.

EMOTIONAL FLOODING 101

When one is flooded by rage, the frontal parts of the brain shut down. Because of this extreme imbalance, the capacity to stand back and observe one's sensations and emotions is lost; rather, one becomes those emotions and sensations.

-Peter A. Levine, PhD. *In an Unspoken Voice: How the Body Releases Trauma and Restores Goodness.* North Atlantic Books, 2010: p. 64.

In part, the Nurtured Heart Approach is a practice of profound noticing. In training ourselves to observe what happens when we encounter something emotionally triggering, to reset ourselves whenever we can, and to intentionally maintain positive interactions and clarity around rules, we develop the ability to prevent the "shutting down" Dr. Levine describes – to maintain our separation from our own sensations and emotions so that they become information rather than overwhelm. In this way, we become empowered in relation to whatever impinges upon us.

Emotional flooding happens when a surge of negative emotion (anger, anxiety, fear, frustration, shame, or a combination of these) triggers a specific cascade of changes in our brains and bodies known as the fight-or-flight response. These physiologic changes temporarily rob us of the ability to use reason and higher intention. They subdue the thinking, decision-making part of the brain in favor of the *limbic* system, the more primitive part of the brain charged with immediate survival. The limbic system includes the *amygdala*, the brain's emotional center, as well as the *hypothalamus*, which is "command central" when it comes to control of heart rate, breathing rate, blood pressure, and the distribution of oxygen-rich blood throughout the body.

Here's how it works:

- You perceive, through your senses, a threat to you or someone you care about.
- A "DANGER" message shoots from the amygdala to the hypothalamus.
- The hypothalamus sends a message hurtling at a speed of 150 meters per second along nerves connected to the adrenals, two walnut-sized glands that sit just above the kidneys. In response, the adrenals dump a hormone called epinephrine, also known as adrenaline, into the circulation.
- Adrenaline floods through the body, raising heart rate, blood pressure, and breathing rate. Blood flow to the internal organs is diverted to the muscles and brain. Stored carbohydrate energy is mobilized from the muscles, raising blood sugar to provide quick energy.
- You fight, flee, or freeze. Hopefully, your reaction is adaptive and helpful for the situation in question. Perhaps fighting is necessary if a dangerous dog attacks you; fleeing is more appropriate if you encounter a threatening stranger in a place where you feel unsafe; and freezing might be the best option if your best bet for remaining safe is to go unseen and unheard.

Everything up to this point happens at lightning speed, which is why you can react so quickly when you perceive danger.

Another important factor in this cascade: while your body is flooded with adrenaline, your higher brain functions go on hold. Critical thinking, logic, consequences and higher intentions all go out the window in favor of quick action and reaction. Sometimes, this is exactly what needs to happen, because lightning-fast decision-making and quick action are vital for survival or safety.

---| MELISSA |--

> One day, when my son Noah was a toddler, I pushed him through a big-box store in a massive cart. He stood up in the front of the cart like Kate Winslet on the prow of the Titanic.
>
> As I strolled and scanned the racks, my peripheral vision caught him toppling headfirst out of the front of the basket toward the polished concrete floor. In the next half-second, I shot belly-first across the length of the big cart and grabbed Noah's ankle as he fell. There he hung, confused, frightened…and safe. It was a super-mom moment – a moment where adrenaline served its rightful purpose.

Imagine if Melissa had paused to consider her options when she saw Noah tumbling toward what might have been his first concussion. Imagine being in a crosswalk with a car bearing down on you and taking the time to muse upon the best course of action. If your house were on fire, you would not stop and pack a healthy breakfast before fleeing.

The concepts of 'emotional flooding' and 'body clues/body signals' are drawn from the AHA! Method, a social-emotional learning curriculum created by Jennifer Freed, PhD, and Rendy Freedman, MFT, founders and co-directors of Santa Barbara, California-based AHA! (Attitude. Harmony. Achievement.), a non-profit that serves 3000+ teens per year.

THE EMOTIONAL FLOODING RESPONSE:

FACE: COMMUNICATES FEAR/ PROTECTIVENESS

THYROID: METABOLISM INCREASES

LUNGS/ HEART: INCREASED OXYGENATION

GASTROINTESTINAL FUNCTION SLOWS
(TUMMY ACHES, IBS)

EXECUTIVE FUNCTION SLOWS
OR ABSENT

Where actual danger is present, you need this response. If you or your loved one is in immediate danger, your thinking brain isn't much use. You want that limbic fight-or-flight response to kick in – to flood your system with adrenaline so that you can get yourself or the other person out of harm's way. Even then, sometimes, that system can kick in so strongly that it impedes the ability to respond in an emergency. This can be especially true for people who did not have good models for emotional regulation in early childhood.

During the flood, the limbic brain sends out loud messages that *handling this issue is the absolute most important thing right now*. It feels like life or death. Your limbic, fight-or-flight brain doesn't know any better, and the logical part of your brain that does *know* better is offline. **Learning to reset yourself is a process of learning to recruit the thinking brain back into service when this happens, and recognizing**

that, until we feel that part of ourselves back online, we should not try to fix, control, or otherwise affect the current situation.

Most of us don't reserve fight/flight/freeze reactions for actual danger. We react to disagreements, problems at work, traffic, and misbehaving children as *though they were dangerous situations*. The fight/flight override can happen in response to even minor irritations. Sometimes we even manage to work ourselves into an emotional flood when *nothing is going wrong*, just because we are projecting into the future or telling ourselves stories that are opposite to the Toll Taker ideal. We can spin ourselves into a reactive frenzy with these stories.

WHEN DANGER ISN'T REALLY DANGEROUS: SOCIAL AND INTERPERSONAL HARM AND THE BACKFIRE EFFECT

Some threats that trigger emotional flooding are "real," meaning that there is actual risk to life or limb. For most of us, threat is perceived more often in terms of our own lifelong beliefs around safety, security, status, ego, or identity — beliefs that feel central to who we are. Such threats feel truly dangerous, bringing up intense fear, anger, frustration, shame, embarrassment, or other challenging emotions. This is why Lindsey panics when she perceives a rupture in the connection with her children, and why Melanie feels afraid when someone portrays her involvement in a situation inaccurately.

Brain research shows that social and interpersonal harm are processed via the same nervous system channels as physical harm. For most of human history, social rejection has been a threat to much more than our emotional health. Belonging to and being accepted by our "tribe" was essential for survival. Although we might now be much better able to meet our own basic survival needs without the support of community, other research shows that the loneliness that comes with standing on our own is as dangerous to our health as a 15-cigarette-a-day smoking habit.[5] The fear, rage, and shame that come up in response to rejection, separation, gaslighting, or other social cues make biologic sense. Still, when we unskillfully respond to these emotions, we often widen the gaps we are trying to close.

An emotional firestorm can erupt in a person who is not in any real danger, but whose belief system is being threatened. We've all seen it happen in others and we've all seen it in ourselves. In the political climate that existed during the writing of this book, we've seen people get triggered well beyond reason by social media arguments about this or that candidate or policy. This isn't to say that certain candidates or policies do not pose true danger to some people; still, reacting to words on a computer screen in a Facebook or online article comment thread as though they were an emergency really doesn't serve anyone or solve any problems.

A blogpost by Matthew Inman entitled "You're not going to believe what I'm about to tell you" (http://theoatmeal.com/comics/believe) illustrates this brilliantly.

It explains the *backfire effect,* which activates the most emotional, reactive part of the brain (the amygdala) in response to information that threatens our core beliefs. The backfire effect is protective in that our worldviews give us all a sense of stability and safety in our complex lives. Having a key part of that worldview challenged, Inman says, is like having a wall knocked out of the house of your worldview, sending the fight/flight/freeze systems into high alert. Potent chemicals produced by those systems activate the body, and before we know it, that Facebook comment

---

[5]   https://www.theguardian.com/commentisfree/2016/oct/12/neoliberalism-creating-loneliness-wrenching-society-apart

has us seeing red and acting in ways that we later regret, or that get us into trouble with people we care about.

This backfire effect can easily arise in parenting, as most of us have a lot of dearly held beliefs about how children should behave and what is and is not acceptable. Many of those beliefs were constructed unconsciously, in our own early childhoods, based on what our own parents taught us both implicitly (through their ways of relating with us) and explicitly (through means like teaching, lectures, sermons, praise, and punishments). Reactivity around certain behaviors of our children can roar up strongly because of these core beliefs in ourselves.

Know that having your beliefs threatened can be a significant trigger and try to notice it when it happens. Practice resetting yourself. Inman does it by "pretending the amygdala of my brain is in my little toe…when a core belief is challenged, I imagine it yelling insane things at me. I let it yell. I let it have its moment." And then, he chooses to remember love, harmony, and beauty. Learning to reset ourselves allows us to take in new information and perspectives. This, in turn, allows us to grow and hold more complex, sophisticated points of view.

What will be your reset when your amygdala wants you to go to war over a belief?

Remnants of parents' own childhood challenges also impact their ability to reset. Having a mentally ill mother created certain triggers within Melanie that elicit a fast fight-or-flight response. Lindsey's experience facing her father's illness and seeing the impact of caregiving on her mother created triggers within her as well.

| MELANIE |

When I enter a plane, I become completely sure that the people assigned to take care of me will kill me. I would pretty much rather not travel anywhere, anytime, than to go through those panicky feelings. It is as charged for me as the most reactive times with my family. There are times that I get so flooded while flying that I stop experiencing what is actually happening. I feel any change in altitude as a crashing drop. I feel slight bumps as terrifyingly extreme. It is amazing how my internally overwrought state can impact my perception of reality while in the air – or while parenting my children.

Through doing this self-regulation work, I can feel this reactivity starting to shift in all areas of my life – not just while flying. I can feel myself give up the fight for my perspective for longer periods of time. Bit by bit, I let myself surrender to trust and faith, to the belief that I am okay—and that I can trust the pilot when flying, or the relationship when on the ground.

I see that this is what's required for my reactive brothers and sisters. We must talk ourselves down. We must be our own best friends. We must fight for reality and for regulation. This is, I believe, the only way to live, and the only way to love.

In situations where life and limb are not at risk, this physical response can interfere with our ability to perceive the reality of the threat, not to mention our ability to creatively address it. If we go into fight-flight-freeze in response to something posing a genuine threat to our child, this system is serving its rightful purpose. Where it tends to be far less helpful is as a response to our child's challenging behaviors.

MANAGING The FLOOD

Adrenaline is active until broken down and processed by the liver and kidneys. If the perceived danger does not continue, this takes at least a few minutes. If the perceived danger continues, or if you ruminate upon the danger and focus on it enough to keep yourself in fight-or-flight, the feedback loop can continue for quite a while. If you are flooded with adrenaline, you are in a reactive state, out of touch with your higher intentions and intelligence, operating in fight/flight/freeze mode. Once flooded, you may need 20 minutes or more to fully reset. You can impact the speed with which you come out of fight-or-flight through cultivating a clean, fast reset to Stand 2.

The keys to managing this are:

1. **To learn to recognize the very earliest signs that the flood is coming, and practice the reset** *then* **– before it happens.** Your body gives you signals that, if you are receptive to them, will help you keep the floodgates closed. Most of us can develop an understanding of our own triggers that will help us reset and keep our thinking brains online even before we begin to experience those body signals.

2. **To develop the ability to recognize when we** *are* **flooded, and to do whatever is necessary to pause** – to *not* act, not make decisions, perhaps not even speak – **until we can reset ourselves.**

EMOTIONS AS ENERGY

Most of us are accustomed to viewing certain emotions, like fear, anger, shame, and frustration, as negative. Our thresholds for tolerating emotions like these tend to be low and our tools for coping with and directing them constructively are usually limited. Most of us didn't grow up with adults in our lives who could help us see that all emotions, even difficult ones, carry gifts and bestow opportunities for growth. Most of us have developed habitual reactions to these emotions, usually grounded in a desire to feel *some other way* as quickly as possible. **While we may need this ability to distract ourselves from or avoid strong emotions at certain times, let's imagine how we**

might work through them transformationally in moments when we can do so without harm to ourselves or others.

The Nurtured Heart Approach tells us to play with experiencing all emotions, "good" and "bad," purely as energy that arises in the body, and to notice how that energy feels – to be present with it – instead of reacting or acting in response to it. Once we have cultivated this skill, we can begin to develop the skill of moving that energy into supporting our higher intentions.

A 2013 study by Finnish researchers Lauri Nummenmaa, Enrico Glerean, Riitta Hari, and Jari Hietanen illustrates the truth of emotions as energy: they asked subjects to draw maps of the places in their bodies where they felt both basic and complex emotions (basic: anger, fear, disgust, happiness, sadness; complex: anxiety, love, depression, contempt, pride, shame, envy). The body maps subjects drew were consistent across different subjects — they mostly reported feeling the same body sensations with the same emotions — and across cultures.

Consider, too, how the omnipresence of emotions in the whole body, not just in the mind, is reflected the language we use to talk about emotions. When we're really feeling something strongly, we tend to describe it in physical terms: *pain in the neck, bent out of shape, coming apart at the seams, heartbroken, head over heels in love, sick to my stomach, made my flesh crawl, out of my head, tearing my hair out, tongue-tied, weak at the knees.*

In a world where we tend to treat the body as mostly a vehicle for the head (with some utility as an object to decorate and admire), this notion of emotions as energy in the body is new to many people... and it is the first and most important step toward becoming more emotionally intelligent.

Most of us learn to tamp down that awareness — to put it aside because it can get in the way and make getting things done more challenging. But when you start to tune into the body sensations that constantly move through you, you may be astonished at the ways in which your life changes. You become more mindful; more grounded; more attuned to the world around you; more present in your relationships. Start talking about these sensations and awarenesses with people who matter to you. Model this for your children.

Start with simple noticing: the next time you feel an emotion you might have considered to be negative, try to experience it as just energy. Notice where you feel that energy in your body. Notice your internal resistance to just letting it be what it is, and notice how it expresses itself: maybe as a hot, buzzy feeling on the crown of your head, a pounding in your chest, or:

- shortness of breath or a sense of being unable to catch your breath
- butterflies in your stomach
- a twitching in your lip or other part of your face
- tightness in your stomach, chest, shoulders, or buttocks
- suddenly wanting to get away or even run
- rapid blinking
- arms activated like they want to throw or hit something

These sensations can show up in an infinite number of ways and combinations; sometimes, they can be surprising. People who are uncomfortable with emotions or who have experienced severe trauma might feel nothing when emotions come up – just numbness or dissociation. If that is true for you, try to notice that. That is how the energy of emotions shows up in your body right now.

Start to notice the energy of difficult emotions when it is moving or stuck in your body. Begin to regard the appearance of these sensations as your cue to reset. Even if nothing seems to be going wrong – if the conversation is calm and no one is breaking any rules – honor those signals as your body's deepest energetic wisdom. Begin to develop a habit of taking the reset well before the flood. With time and practice, you will develop the skill of intentionally moving that energy into Stand 2 (recognitions, gratitude, appreciation) – directing its intensity and strength toward greatness.

IDENTIFYING "BODY SIGNALS"

This is a brief exercise to help you begin to notice the need for a reset long before you become reactive in a way that sabotages your use of the Nurtured Heart Approach.

Think about a time you lost it – where you couldn't have regained control in the moment if your life depended on it. Maybe you said or did something you regretted and wish you could take back. Write it down.

Notice how reminiscing about what happened brings up sensations in your body. Those sensations are important clues that will help you later when we start to look at tools for better emotional management. Scan your body with your attention from the soles of your feet to the crown of your head, and write down those sensations in as much detail as you can:

Example: When I remember _____ (that time I yelled "F---- you!" at my husband), *I feel* _____ (a fluttering in my solar plexus, and a tingling on the top of my head, my heart beating and sweaty palms).

Take note of these sensations. They are your body's signal that you are about to become flooded. In general, begin to pay attention to your body sensations; pay special attention in challenging moments.

Some people who are especially challenged by strong emotions – in particular, those who have experienced significant trauma (more on this in the next chapter) – may not be able to identify these kinds of body signals. They may just feel a numbness or a sense of being frozen. If this seems true for you, start to notice when that numb feeling arises. That may be your clearest body signal, for now.

Knowing what signals your body usually sends out just before the flood will help you recognize when it's time to reset: to step back, withdraw your energy, and focus on moving that intensity into Stand 2 and into greatness rather than going down the road of negativity. As you become more aware, you will learn to detect them long before they knock you out of your commitment to refuse to energize negativity.

Behaviors as Signals of a Coming Flood

Sometimes, the flood can take us by surprise. In order to function well in the face of strong emotions, most of us developed self-soothing strategies or go-to behaviors early in life that dissociate or dampen our internal awareness of our own feeling states. While some of these default behaviors – which, are in essence, attempts at self-resets – might be more helpful than harmful, some (as you'll see below) could stand to be examined and replaced with more positive modes of resetting. Catching ourselves in behaviors or tendencies like the ones listed below can help bring more awareness to that important moment before the flood, where a thorough self-reset can do the most good. With practice, most everyone can learn to recognize internal energetic shifts; but the first step for some may be to notice certain behavioral cues as times to check in with themselves, notice clues in their bodies, and reset before the flood.

A reset is probably called for if you find yourself:

- Craving or overconsuming foods you know are bad for your health
- Needing or consuming an alcoholic drink, something sweet, or some other mind-altering substance to manage your mood
- Picking at your cuticles or skin or engaging in other kinds of self-harm
- Having trouble focusing or staying present in a conversation
- Picking fights or trying to create other kinds of interpersonal drama

- Over-exercising or not wanting to exercise at all (if you usually do exercise)
- Complaining, gossiping, or telling tales of how others have done you wrong
- Spending excessive time surfing the Web or watching television
- Falling into patterns of addictive behavior (regardless of the addiction)

These are a few of the ways people try to stuff or ignore their emotions, and that can lead to an emotional upheaval that sabotages the First Stand.

WAYS TO RESET WHEN THE FLOOD HAS ALREADY ARRIVED

While resetting before the flood is the ideal, let's acknowledge that it is not always possible. Knowing this, learn to recognize when you are flooded, and that you can choose to pause and calm yourself down before you respond to the situation you are in. Here are a few research-proven suggestions for calming yourself out of fight-flight-freeze mode and into a space where a true reset is possible.

Once you recognize you are flooded, step away from the issue/problem at hand. Don't in any way give your energy to negativity. Work to actively refuse to spin out mentally about the triggering situation; if this is not possible for you, build awareness that the spin is fight-or-flight energy that can be waited out before taking action. Distract yourself if necessary (see ideas for this below). Hold onto Stand 1 as though your life depended on it. Unless someone is in immediate danger, turn away; walk away; hand the situation over to someone else. Take 20 minutes to reset if possible.

Try to remember that when you get crazed and feel your heart race, breath shorten, thoughts race, a scream in your throat, *your body is in an emergency state.* While flooded, be wary of impulses to convince yourself that you are correct in your crazed feeling, and that if you were just listened to, you would feel right and good again. You cannot handle a non-emergency situation with intelligence or perspective if you are internally in a state of emergency, as your brain is only capable of processing extreme, "black-and-white" options. Take time and space to regain love and compassion for both you and the other person. From that place, you can get back in touch with the higher thinking centers of the brain and start again.

Learn to feel when you're back online. Check in: do you feel the warm glow of love inside you again, toward the person whose behavior who has triggered you? If you feel love, you are reset. Has your heart rate slowed? Have your urges to run or fight faded? Do you feel calm? Happy? Connected? Are you able to acknowledge that someone else has a valid point of view? Can you feel grateful for the things you *could* have done while flooded but wisely didn't? Has your body relaxed? Has your face softened? These are good indications that you have reset successfully. As soon as you are reset, dive back into your Stands.

At first, the self-reset after the flood may be primarily a matter of waiting quietly and self-soothing in very basic ways, many of which we will discuss later in this book; but as you develop and practice your NHA skills, you will find that moving the energy of difficult emotions into Stand 2 recognitions will help you take control of this process and move more quickly into desirable emotional states that are conducive to parenting with intention.

As you practice this way of being in a challenging situation, you train your observing, decision-making, mindful prefrontal cortex to stay online even as you harbor what Peter Levine, PhD calls "raw, primitive sensations generated in archaic portions of the brain" (the limbic brain, the hypothalamus and the brainstem).[6]

FROM FLOOD TO STEADY TRICKLE: THE CORTISOL RESPONSE

If you do not manage stress proactively, your body may decide that fight-or-fight adrenaline bursts aren't efficient enough. Where danger persists, a longer-term stress response involving your adrenal

---

[6] Levine, Peter A., PhD. In an Unspoken Voice: How the Body Releases Trauma and Restores Goodness. North Atlantic Books, 2010: p. 71.

glands and the hormone cortisol creates continual alertness and energy so that you can do what's necessary to restore yourself or your loved ones to safety:

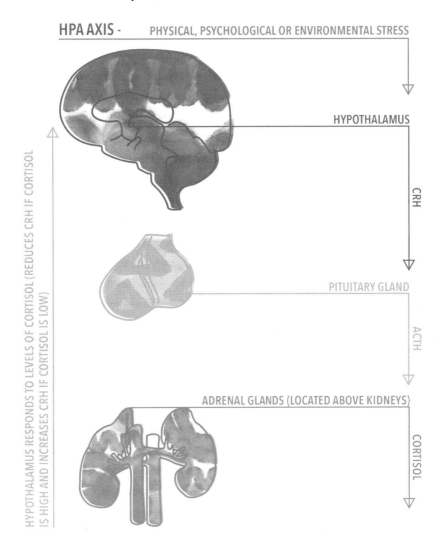

1. The hypothalamus releases *corticotropin releasing hormone* (CRH). When CRH hits the pituitary gland, it triggers a release of *adrenocorticotropic hormone* (ACTH). ACTH travels to the adrenal glands through the circulation.

2. CRH stimulates the adrenals to release a hormone called *cortisol,* which keeps the body at a level of high alert – but not at fight-or-flight levels. Heart rate, blood pressure, breathing rate, blood sugar, and alertness stay elevated over time.

If the adrenaline response is like slamming down the gas pedal and then letting it go, this other response is like keeping the gas pedal pressed down partway. In a cortisol-elevated state, we are more easily kicked back into emotional flooding and tend to catastrophize and look for fault. We have fewer resources for parenting, living, and relating with positive intention. Eventually, we become exhausted.

Heightened cortisol does not necessarily interfere with clear higher-level thinking in the moment – in fact, cortisol enhances quick thinking and reasoning – but over time, chronically high cortisol sets us up for depression, anxiety, and even memory loss. Elevated cortisol levels are predictive of lower life expectancy, and can harm immune function, bone density, body weight, blood pressure, and heart health.

Think of someone you know for whom every busted taillight is a ten-car pile-up waiting to happen; for whom every sideways look is a condemnation or criticism; for whom the worst outcome is always expected. That person is probably hopped up on a heady mix of cortisol and adrenaline. So is the person who seems to thrive on intense work stresses – who is overly busy and overcommitted, but seems to think that this lack of self-care and downtime is an immovable part of who they are.

Many of us are stuck in a cortisol-elevated state. The American Psychology Association's annual stress survey shows that at least ¼ of Americans experience high ongoing levels of stress (eight or more on a ten-point scale) and that half experience moderate levels (between four and seven on the same scale).

We can change this with awareness and a shift in our thoughts and habits. NHA techniques are great for stress reduction, both in the moment (preventing unnecessary or counterproductive adrenaline flooding) and longer-term (keeping cortisol within healthy limits). Learning to reset yourself, seeing the good and cultivating gratitude, and building clear structure and boundaries all bring inner peace and peace in relationships – the opposite of emotional flooding and cortisol overload.

BALANCING THE NERVOUS SYSTEM

The human nervous system has two "branches": the *sympathetic* nervous system (SNS) and the *parasympathetic* nervous system (PNS). The SNS is about fight, flight or freeze responses, as well as about being able to achieve, do, conquer fear, and meet challenges; and the PNS is all about resting and digesting, tending and befriending.

These two branches work best when kept in balance: enough risk, challenge, and adventure, balanced by stress management and plenty of down time and self-care. To set the stage for more immediate emotional

 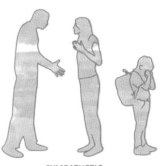

	PARASYMPATHETIC	SYMPATHETIC
GENERAL FUNCTION	MAINTAIN BALANCED FUNCTION THROUGHOUT THE BODY; "REST AND DIGEST"	RESPOND TO DANGER OR STRESS; "FIGHT OR FLIGHT"
GENERAL BODY RESPONSE	CONTROL THE BODY'S RESPONSE WHILE AT REST	BODY SPEEDS UP, TENSES UP, BECOMES MORE ALERT. FUNCTIONS NOT CRITICAL TO SURVIVAL SHUT DOWN
CARDIOVASCULAR SYSTEM	DECREASES HEART RATE	INCREASES MUSCULAR CONTRACTION, HEART RATE
PULMONARY SYSTEM	BRONCHIAL TUBES CONSTRICT	BRONCHIAL TUBES DILATE
MUSCULOSKELETAL SYSTEM	MUSCLES RELAX	MUSCLES CONTRACT
PUPILS	CONSTRICT	DILATE
GASTROINTESTINAL SYSTEM	INCREASES STOMACH MOVEMENT AND SECRETIONS	DECREASES STOMACH MOVEMENT AND SECRETIONS

management – to manage triggers – do things every day to activate your PNS: meditation, progressive relaxation, yoga, deep breathing, gratitude practices, moderate physical exercise, being in nature, and other soothing activities. Like a muscle, the PNS becomes more "toned" with more use. People who practice yoga or meditation regularly are less susceptible to being triggered into a state of emotional flooding.

The greater your parasympathetic tone, the higher your flooding threshold will be. If you do not yet have a regular mindfulness practice in place, let this be your motivation to begin. Ongoing practice, even for a few minutes a day, will enhance your PNS tone. Refer to Chapter Seven, "Ways to Reset (A Partial List)," for more on this.

WHY STRESS CAN BE ADDICTING

The heightened, stressed-out states described in this chapter can feel good! People can get hooked on these states of being. They can even be addictive.

When we are highly stressed or in pain, the body produces *endorphins,* opiate-like natural chemicals that help us bear what might otherwise seem unbearable. Those of us who seek out risk, drama and danger may keep going back to those situations to feel that flood of endorphins. Part of the reason self-harm feels "good" to those who do it is the fact that it triggers endorphin production. There is a kind of "being present" that comes only in high-stress moments, and that can be addicting as well. Being chronically stressed, rushed, and aggravated can help us avoid feelings or thoughts that seem too difficult to face.

Modern cultures celebrate people for being overly busy and high-achieving. Children and teens easily get the impression that if they aren't stressed, they aren't doing enough. The popularity of negative drama has much to do with the fact that it can quickly, reliably create a palpable physical and psychological rush.

We are not suggesting a life free of drama. The key is to let the drama happen around what is going well instead of what is going wrong!

| MELANIE |

My mother, in her rage, taught me how to fight back. I needed that ability to survive my childhood. From living this out without awareness in my own parenting, I have created two children who are real fighters. I had to wake up one day, become acutely aware of what I was passing on, and say, *the legacy stops here*. I took on the responsibility to teach them better ways to respond to difficulty than those I had learned under extreme duress in my own childhood.

In my quest for effective guidance about how to parent, I've felt frustrated by how many models for parenting assume that all parents have an innate capacity for balance and self-control. I would read all these great books, thinking: *there is no way I can implement this fantastic advice while I remain as challenged with emotional regulation as my children.*

When I started working with the Nurtured Heart world, I felt that my fallibility, my struggle to reset, was an accepted part of this process. Through commitment and hard work, I've reached a place where I can always reset. There is always safe ground to which I can return. Wherever my flailing takes me, it's always *en route* back to that place of being reset and remembering how I want to show up for my children, and everyone else in my life…myself included. Always remembering that refusing to energize my family negatively—refusing to criticize, while dedicating myself to finding every grain of goodness in them—is the one immediate and long-range way to teach my children self-regulation. This is how to instill self-confidence and self-love in them, and how to maintain a bond where we can always come back together, throughout all the mistakes and missteps.

I grew up in the flood. I've learned to love myself in the

flood. I'm still knee-deep in it much of the time. I don't kid myself that the flood will ever subside completely. However: I'm growing myself up, right here, in the thick of it.

Our children are 100% our spiritual teachers. When my children are pushing me to my limit, how can I be anything but grateful that they are giving me more opportunity to be a better, more patient, thoughtful human? This thought won't always be something that helps me reset in a reactive moment, but it's one that is always there for me to return to as soon as I reach for it.

CHAPTER FOUR

RESTORING THE PRESENT,

Releasing the Past: Early Childhood Attachment and Emotional Management

I have been fascinated with how the blueprint of core beliefs is already actively shaping babies' lives in terms of their physical structure, physiology, their relationship to self, others, and to the world as well... Although these early belief blueprints can become entrenched and continue for a lifetime, when brought to awareness and worked with directly, they are quite changeable.

- Wendy McCarty, PhD (2002)

Learning about emotional flooding and figuring out when and how to calm ourselves down to reset successfully are both aspects of emotional management: the ability to feel our emotions fully without reacting to them or from them in destructive ways. Good emotional management is what enables us to consistently maintain the Three Stands of the Nurtured Heart Approach.

Emotional management is one facet of emotional intelligence (EQ), which was brought into the psychology mainstream by psychologist and journalist Daniel Goleman, PhD. He defines EQ as **the ability to recognize, understand, and manage our own emotions and to recognize, understand, and influence the emotions of others.** Others have included in the definition of emotional intelligence the ability to harness emotions and apply them to tasks like thinking and problem solving.[7]

---

[7] Psychology Today, https://www.psychologytoday.com/basics/emotional-intelligence, accessed 8/7/16

What might make a person's success at managing anger, fear or anxiety a cause for celebration rather than just business as usual? Why might some people have to fight that much harder to keep their cool?

The most likely possibilities:

1. **Life stresses.**
2. **Health issues.**
3. **Native intensity.**
4. **Disruptions in healthy early childhood attachment.**
5. **Traumatic childhood experiences.**

The first two factors in this list happen for all of us. When we have too much on our plates or don't feel well, resetting can be a bigger challenge. With life stresses, it's not really a question of *whether* they will impact our ability to avoid emotional flooding; it's a question of *when*. If you sense that people in general are mightily stressed these days, it's not just your imagination; and if you feel you're experiencing more stress in your life than is healthy or wholesome, that's probably the truth for you.

A study published in late 2017 by the American Psychological Association surveyed the state of the U.S. in terms of stress and its impacts. Researchers polled 1,376 men and 2,047 women over age 18 from across the nation. The results: we are at a 4.8 on a 1-10 scale nationwide (no differences between areas of the U.S.) More respondents than ever before reported that the stress they experienced was impacting their ability to sleep well and to feel calm and peaceful during the day. A third of subjects reported feeling nervousness, anxiety, irritability, anger, or fatigue as a result of being stressed. Seventy-five percent of respondents said they'd had at least one symptom of acute stress (those consistent with post-traumatic stress disorder) during the month before taking the survey.

We aren't meaning to stress you further by pointing out the fact that so many of us are living with high, potentially toxic levels of stress! We simply mean to normalize that everyone can sometimes struggle to regulate themselves when emotions run high. Stress lowers our thresholds, but the hopeful news is that the Nurtured Heart Approach is a wonderful stress-reducing strategy that incorporates mindfulness and gratitude. When applied with intention, it solves stressful problems (such as a child's challenging behavior) and in reducing our focus on problems in general. As we develop the skills needed to move the energy of stress into Stands One and Two, we can transmute that energy into something nourishing and supportive. If the third factor is in play for you or a child of yours, you know firsthand that this is just how some of us come in. Those of us who come into this lifetime as a VW Bug with a Maserati engine possess power and intensity that can generate magic – and that may also threaten the ability of the chassis to hold together from time to time.

The remainder of this chapter will look at the first of the last two factors; the chapter following will examine the final factor in this list. Both can create unconscious emotional patterns that sabotage great parenting intentions. Both are far more common than you might think.

Even if you think you had a perfect childhood, read and consider this chapter and the next. You may recognize yourself in some important ways. You may also recognize behaviors your children have displayed that previously seemed mystifying (for example, excessive 'clinginess,' reluctance to share honestly about tough emotions or try new things, or difficulty moving through challenging emotional states). One of the most important influences on your own parenting were your own earliest experiences being parented, and it's possible that you have played out some of the less constructive aspects of that parenting without realizing it, even if you have wanted desperately to improve on what you experienced. These influences from our own parenting easily become second nature, like software running in the background of our lives without our awareness.

In some instances, we may develop a habit of doing the opposite of what our parents did – unconsciously reacting to what we didn't like or what felt wrong to us in those relationships. The common denominator is that unconscious reactivity is calling the shots. Awakening our awareness of these patterns is the first step in developing the ability to parent responsively rather than reactively.

Disruptions in healthy early childhood attachment and traumatic childhood experiences impact us at the deepest level, below the level of the thinking brain, deep down in the limbic system and amygdala. They may become integrated into our behaviors at the level of implicit memory – pre-language memories largely built in the first year and a half or so of life – before we even have language to describe them.

Habitual, reactive ways of handling and expressing emotions that come from early childhood feel automatic, like default settings – until we have the knowledge we need to recognize that (1) these patterns are learned, not inborn, and (2) once recognized, they can be worked with and shifted.

These chapters are meant to gently awaken you to any "stuck" energy that has worked against your ability to parent responsively instead of reactively. We'll "name it to tame it" – identify what old energetic realities might be hiding behind the scenes, making present emotional management harder. And the beauty of the inner application of the Nurtured Heart Approach is that whether or not we know the source of the energy from the past that is bringing up reactivity in the present, that energy can be used and repurposed to grow the greatness of responsiveness.

The material in these chapters should also help you more clearly identify what kinds of situations are your strongest triggers for emotional states that work against your parenting intentions. Knowing these triggers will help you recognize them farther in advance, and you can see and use them as cues to reset. As you will see, these energies can ultimately be useful.

Early Attachment, EQ,
and Emotional Management

EQ and emotional management are not inborn skills. Ideally, we learn them in very early life, through direct experiences with caregivers.

If parents are a child's favorite toy, they are their infant's best chance at survival. In the first months of life, having our needs for nourishment, warmth, and loving interaction met is a matter of life and death. Everything about an infant's behavior is meant to trigger parental instincts toward protecting and loving that child. The child is geared to respond to any sign of parental discomfort or rejection with behaviors that will keep the parent close. This is the dance of attachment. The way attachment plays out in the first 18 months of life has powerful impact on the ways we relate to others throughout the rest of our lives and on the way we end up parenting our own children.

Every child has a primary caregiver during most of this time – usually, the mother. This caregiver's way of relating to the young child dictates the way the child attaches to them. The study of this process of attachment – and its ramifications over lifetimes — is known as *attachment theory.*[8]

Attachment begins as the newborn's immediate needs for nourishment, comfort, sleep, and high-quality parent-child bonding are either consistently or inconsistently met. As the child grows and begins to explore the world, they continue to need their parents to create a secure base that they can trust to return to when they need reassurance and support. They need to observe their caregivers being able to feel, manage, and express their own emotions in healthy ways, and to provide guidance for the child in managing theirs.

Young children's explorations often lead them to fear, anger, frustration, or disappointment. To generate a healthy attachment, parents must consistently see and honor these emotions, reflect them accurately, and provide comfort and soothing to the child. Over time, children learn that they can handle difficulty, feel and trust their emotions, and venture forth once more. Parents who can remain calm and balanced while feeling rage, helplessness, fear, or frustration teach their children that they can be (1) highly emotionally activated, (2) safe, and (3) beloved – all at the same time.

---

[8] This is often confused with the set of behaviors known collectively as attachment parenting, where parents hold, feed, and relate to an infant not on a schedule or per parental dictates but in consistent response to the child's cues. Co-sleeping – sleeping with the infant for at least the first year of life or beyond – is part of the rubric of attachment parenting. This way of parenting an infant does not work for everyone, and it is not necessary for good attachment.

Through being aware of and responsive to the very young child – a state of being called *attunement* – the parent can sense when the child needs support and comfort and when she needs to be allowed to explore. When attunement does not happen, or when it happens inconsistently or less constructively, this attachment bond may form in ways that negatively affect the child's behavior and emotional development in predictable ways. The ability to attune is not inborn, either – it's learned primarily in the process of having others attune to us when we are small. It can be learned in adulthood through mindful parenting of our own children. (This is one way in which the Nurtured Heart Approach fosters healthy attachment: it encourages a profound level of attachment.)[9]

WE ALL DO THE BEST WE CAN

Modern life tends to be rushed and stressful even without adding children to the mix. When a primary caregiver is called to do it all – to parent, to maintain a home, and maybe also to maintain a professional life – creating ideal levels of attunement and attachment can be a real challenge. Any additional stressful factor can amplify the difficulty a primary caregiver faces in being fully present for and emotionally regulated with their child. The circumstances in which we find ourselves as modern parenting humans are radically different and radically more time-condensed and stressful than most that have existed in any time in our history on this planet. Our attention and energy are pulled in many directions virtually all the time.

If you recognize that you were not as able to attune with or emotionally regulate around your child in their earliest months and years as you would have liked, trust that there was good reason for this, and that you did the best you could do with the resources you possessed. Say "Absolutely No" to any sense of self-blame or self-shaming around

---

[9] Material on attachment theory throughout this chapter is sourced primarily from the work of Bert Powell, Glen Cooper, Kent Hoffman, and Bob Marvin, creators of the Circle of Security Intervention and authors of The Circle of Security Intervention: Enhancing Attachment in Early Parent-Child Relationships .The Guilford Press, 2014.

this and remind yourself that now, you are living out the greatness of determination, curiosity, self-examination, and the desire to become the best parent you can be. This goes for your parents, as well.

Most adults reading this book will find themselves at some point in a process of recognizing that their own parents may not have done their jobs perfectly, and that the impact of these parents' choices may have created challenges for them in their own adult lives and in their own parenting. Our hope is that the material presented here will help move you to a place of compassion and forgiveness for any such choices your parents made when you were small. We will, in fact, show you how to channel that energy into even more greatness.

SECURE ATTACHMENT AND EMOTIONAL EDUCATION

Attachment is one specific and circumscribed aspect of the relationship between a child and caregiver that is involved with making the child safe, secure and protected. The purpose of attachment is not to play with or entertain the child…feed the child…set limits for the child…or teach the child new skills. Attachment is where the child uses the primary caregiver as a secure base from which to explore and, when necessary, as a haven of safety and a source of comfort.

- Diane Benoit, MD, FRCPC; Paediatrics and Child Health, 2004 Oct; 9(8): 541-5.

When this secure base (the adult who encourages the child to explore, with reassurance that they are there for the child during this process) and safe haven (the adult who is available to comfort and encourage the child when they are experiencing challenging emotions) are consistently offered, the child develops a *secure attachment style*. A recent study of about 2,000 infants tested with the gold-standard research tool (the Strange Situation test[10]) demonstrated that about 55 percent were securely attached in their relationships to their primary caregivers. They come to know they can safely learn and explore and can count on a reliable, warm, supportive parental presence when they need a safe harbor for re-fueling, emotional support, and further exploration. No parent is *perfectly* responsive or attuned; if the secure base and safe haven are offered consistently, that's what matters.

In NHA terms, the child acutely discerns, at an energetic level, whether the parent's attunement, connection and appreciation are reliable. Knowing that this safe harbor is reliably present gives the child 'wings' – the basis upon which they can be there for themselves and venture securely into the world.

Secure attachment gives the young child the best potential for emotional intelligence and good emotional management. A parent who can help the child manage the emotions that come up in the context of exploration is a parent who can tolerate feeling those same emotions. The child trusts that they can express challenging emotions and receive comfort in response. They begin, in early life, to learn to self-regulate strong reactions and emotions with adult support. A parent who can model the ability to feel all kinds of emotions fully and to be a constant and accepting presence in the child's world as they feel them is more likely to build a secure attachment with the child.

The very young child whose parent sets an example of emotional intelligence within a secure attachment learns that their own challenging feelings are valid; that they provide them with important information that helps them make choices; and that they will pass. The child knows that if they become distressed while exploring their world, they can count on the caregiver to offer comfort and safety until they are OK to start exploring again. In being consistently soothed, they learn to self-soothe.

---

[10] The Strange Situation test places a child (usually aged between ages 12 and 20 months) in a playroom with his primary caregiver, who then leaves the room, leaving the child alone with a stranger. The caregiver then re-enters the playroom and the child's responses are carefully observed and recorded. This cycle is repeated twice. Over years of study and thousands upon thousands of Strange Situation tests, its creators have developed the ability to identify four specific attachment types in these parent-child relationships: secure, anxious/avoidant, anxious/ambivalent (all organized forms of attachment) and disorganized. Long-term studies correlate these types with outcomes in later childhood, adulthood, and even in the eventual parenting styles of those who were tested with their own parents in childhood.

The Nurtured Heart Approach offers a reliable set of guidelines for building and maintaining secure attachment. For those who use it diligently, a form of attachment that is *beyond* secure seems to emerge. We believe that a big part of the healing possible with this approach comes through mending of insecure or disorganized attachment (both of these are defined below).

INSECURE ATTACHMENT AND EMOTIONAL HEALTH

When either the secure base or safe haven is consistently disrupted, children may develop *insecure* attachment strategies. This is a probable outcome when a child's primary caregiver:

- **Seems consistently uncomfortable with the child expressing emotional distress.** This is likely to lead to *anxious/avoidant* attachment, where the child learns to suppress emotional expression and appear not to need the parent as a safe harbor as much as they actually do.
- **Seems consistently uncomfortable with the child's explorations.** This is likely to lead to *anxious/ambivalent* attachment, where the child learns that the parent "needs to be needed" or is fearful of the child exploring their world. The child learns to act as though they need the parent more than they do and will curtail their explorations to stay close to the caregiver.

Both strategies involve anxiety, because they are motivated by a child's need for their caregiver to stay close and attuned. They are also *organized*, which means that they involve consistent behavior patterns. They are both forms of *insecure attachment*.

According to the Center on the Social and Emotional Foundations for Early Learning, children with insecure attachment relationships may tend to:

- Behave as if they know that adults are inconsistently or seldom available (avoidant)
- Stay close to an adult to get needs met, inhibiting their exploration, or cut short explorations to seek comfort for no

apparent reason (ambivalent)

- Become distressed but do not seek out an adult to help them deal with emotions (avoidant)
- Hide strong feelings and withdraw to avoid distressing events (avoidant)
- Seem clingy and hard to soothe (ambivalent)
- Retreat to try to organize their emotions on their own, thus missing opportunities for emotional education and expression (avoidant)

NO BLAME, NO SHAME

If you recognize patterns here that have impacted your own parenting, pause and take a few deep breaths. Remember that our purpose is to help you reflect on the way you were parented, notice whether you are unconsciously repeating those patterns, and to use that awareness to help you choose differently.

The aim of parents is to keep their children safe. If they adopted an insecure attachment style with their own primary caregiver, they did so because it was the only way they knew to keep their caregiver close and maintain the greatest possible safety. So, they will often unconsciously re-create this same insecure attachment strategy with their children.

If the parent learned from their own primary caregiver that it might not be safe to reveal negative emotions or look to others to support them in navigating those emotions, they may default to a parenting style that discourages this. If their parents seemed most connected to them when they were clingy and needy, they may also act in ways that elicit those responses from their own child. These parenting "moves" are both made from a heartfelt desire to keep the child as safe and protected as possible.

Howard Glasser likes to say that children read energy like Braille – and that they are drawn to what brings them into the most energetically connected relationship. If they don't receive the strongest connection via positivity, they will seek it out through negativity or through other patterns of reactivity that we are exploring here.

MELISSA

I had a good childhood: financial security, comfort, good health; a home filled with laughter and cuddling where no one was cruel or unkind; travel; emphasis on learning and knowledge and a guarantee of four years in college all paid for. And by the time I was in my middle teens, I suffered from depression so extreme that my therapist said, "Not giving her antidepressants would be like not giving insulin to a diabetic."

In all my privilege, I felt lost. I would cry and smash my head against the wall; my guts hurt but there was no physical explanation for the pain; I self-harmed. Sometimes I felt caught up in a weird ecstasy that I couldn't explain. Diagnosed with major depression, I was placed on meds. The side effects were immediate and unacceptable, so I stopped. Still, the belief remained in me that I had an illness – a biochemical imbalance that I would have for the rest of my life.

In my mid-20s, fresh out of grad school, I moved from the east coast to Santa Barbara, California. I began to study all I could about mind/soul/spirit/body integration and indigenous wisdom. I joined a women's circle, studied yoga and eventually became a yoga teacher, wrote my heart open through poetry and prose and spoken-word performance works, danced, and attended personal growth workshops. I learned the Nurtured Heart Approach and embraced it in every aspect of my life. Today, I know I've beat depression for good, and this shift had everything to do with emotional intelligence.

Because of their own upbringings, my wonderful parents had been led to believe that emotions like anger, fear, shame, and grief were best left unexpressed. It was more important to get along than to risk relationship rupture. I had learned, very early in my life, to try to hide difficult emotions from others, and to reject them within myself – they were inconvenient, inconsiderate, and threatening. To be sad or angry would mean hurting others or pushing them away. I learned to leave more difficult emotions unexpressed for the sake of keeping others close. I believe that the anxiety and depression in my family line results directly from this.

Through learning the NHA, I came to recognize that all emotional states need a seat at the table of who I am. I came to see that anger is necessary for the drawing of solid boundaries. I worked hard to get to where I could feel it inside myself without recoiling. I worked even harder to develop ways of expressing anger that were healthy and made my relationships better. Once I began that work, I came to see that beneath much of the anger I felt were sadness and grief. I began to let myself feel these things fully. As I did this, I came to fear others' anger, sadness and grief less.

In learning the NHA and other valuable modes of emotional awareness and expression, and in diligently practicing bringing all my emotional states into my relationships and decision-making, I feel I'm breaking a harmful cycle. My own work on this has enabled me to raise my own children to feel fully. We've made no emotional state off-limits, and I have worked with them to encourage healthy expression and re-purposing of challenging emotional energies. I'm grateful to have learned what I needed to learn to make this happen for them, and I'm grateful for ALL emotions and the gifts they bring.

DISORGANIZED ATTACHMENT

When a parent is abusive, neglectful, dissociated, or highly unpredictable in the ways they respond to the child's needs for closeness or exploration – in other words, where neither safe haven or secure base can be counted on, and where the parent is sometimes actively terrifying to the child – this gives rise to *disorganized* attachment.

A parent who has trouble tolerating their own emotions is unlikely to be able to tolerate them in the child, and that fear in the parent may cause them to behave in ways that scare the child. As a result, the child is wired to go to the parent for comfort, but they are also afraid of the parent. In *The Circle of Attachment Intervention,* the authors cite an extreme example of a young boy who was hospitalized after being set on fire by his mother – and who cried out for her from his hospital bed.

A child with a mentally ill or addicted parent, with a parent who had un-healed loss or trauma or disorganized attachment to their own parent(s), or whose parents have significant marital discord (possibly including marital abuse) is most likely to have this disorganized, confused, fearful default approach to relationship. They are always on alert and easily triggered into "fight, flight, or freeze" mode.[11] Their executive function – their ability to begin tasks, follow through, complete tasks, organize, and be responsible – is likely to suffer, because when we are laser-focused on survival (as we are when we are in fight/flight/freeze mode), we don't have ready access to the part of the brain that acts as the executive arm. When a child is in an overwhelmed state for much of the time, those skills do not develop the way they could if they were secure and calm. Children with this kind of history often struggle to focus and sit still in school and are more likely to receive an ADHD diagnosis than the kind of healing nurturance that could create the sense of safety that could make them able to achieve to their potential. A review of 29 studies on disorganized attachment and later ADHD diagnosis published in 2013 found a significant correlation between these two factors.[12]

---

[11] Wittmer, Donna. Attachment: What Works? The Center on the Social and Emotional Foundations for Early Learning: http://csefel.vanderbilt.edu/resources/wwb/wwb24.html
[12] Storebo, Ole Jakob, Pernille Darling Rasmussen, Erik Simonsen. Association Between Insecure Attachment and ADHD: Environmental Mediating Factors. Journal of Attention Disorders, September 23, 2013.

In the Strange Situation test, the child with disorganized attachment will behave in inexplicable or bizarre ways: they will run to the caregiver upon their return, then run away; they might approach the caregiver backwards, or cling to the caregiver while hitting them or otherwise seeming afraid and resistant.

MICHAEL[13]

My mom had an old-school attitude toward discipline: instilling fear through the constant threat of violence. As a young child, I remember longing for her to nurture me, but having to feel out whether it was safe to approach her. If I misread her, I would be pushed away, hit, or told, "Get away from me!" I remember running up to her one day, excited about something, when she was talking to a neighbor. She hit me so hard I was knocked unconscious. Another time she hit me in the temple with the heel of a high-heeled shoe. And yet another time, when I was in middle school, I was taking the dog out, and I guess I wasn't doing it fast enough, because she stabbed me in the back with a grapefruit knife. I was in the hospital for a few days and was paralyzed from the waist down for two weeks. My parents told me what to tell the people at the hospital so that they wouldn't get in trouble.

If I looked upset or sad I'd hear, "Change the attitude." If I was crying about something, I'd be told, "I'll give you something to cry about." My dad would come home and my mom would say something like, "Michael didn't clean up" or "He was nothing but trouble all day," and Dad would say, "What are you upsetting your mother for?" and I'd be sent off to get the belt.

As an adult, I spent a lot of energy and time trying to understand and forgive my parents. In my intimate

---

[13] In this story, names and details have been changed.

relationships, I have often felt myself wanting to be close and run away at the same time. When I was expected to be most vulnerable, I could feel myself shut down. I have literally run away at times from intimacy. I have problems managing my temper. I'm a big, rugged looking man with a booming voice, and when my anger and meanness burst through, it is scary to the people I love.

I got in a lot of fights and willingly risked my life often over the years; it's a miracle that I'm still here. I'd like to say that I had these experiences because I'm a superhero who shows up to rescue the oppressed and beat down bad guys, but that's not the truth (at least, not the whole truth). I know I created these situations because I couldn't manage my emotions. I didn't know that was something people did. My emotions *were* me, and the bigger they were, the more like myself I felt. They ruled me, and they were unpredictable, sometimes explosive. I'd make things worse on purpose – the thought pattern was something like, "If this is going to be bad, let's make sure it gets as bad as it can get," and I would get to off-gas some of the poison I carried around inside of me.

My executive function – being organized, getting things done on schedule, and being overall responsive and responsible – has been poor. Often, if something I had to do felt triggering emotionally, I would get big and angry or shut down and dissociate and the thing would not get done. I never wanted to ask anyone for help, and I'd break my back trying to be helpful to other people. Self-soothing? Forget it. Trust? The world was obviously out to get me.

I pledged never to have a child of my own. The last thing I wanted to do was pass on whatever I was carrying from the abandonment and abuse I experienced. I knew it would be a lifelong job to try to resolve my own issues and that being a parent would require me to change and heal faster than I thought I could. And then, without intending to, I became a father.

In parenting my now-teenaged son, I am learning along with him how to manage and tolerate all kinds of emotions, how to connect in healthy ways, how to parent non-reactively with good boundaries and healthy attunement, and to manage my life better overall. The more I understand the ways these things impact me, the better able I am to choose the best turns on my healing path. Because I still run the risk of getting so flooded that I can't make good choices, I am always playing around with ideas for how to reset. For a while I had a crystal pendant I wore around my neck that I 'programmed' with statements like "Take the high road" and "Clarity" and "Reset," and I would touch it to remember myself when I'd start to get flooded. I set an alarm four times a day on my iPhone to remind me to ask myself how I'm feeling, which helps me not let anger or sadness build up. I energize myself for successes. I also practice deep breathing in tough moments.

I have high hopes for myself and my beautiful son. Being his dad has inspired me to levels of emotional regulation and aliveness I never knew existed. It has also inspired me to work at learning to soothe myself so I can be there for others, and to build my self-control, mindfulness, and capacity for connection. My gratitude for this, and for him, is boundless.

The parent with this kind of history in their own childhood (like Michael or Melanie) may have to work much harder to keep their cool when parenting their own children. The converse of this can be a tendency to doubt or resist positive connection – a perfectly logical adaptive response for someone who didn't know, in early life, whether attempts to connect would bring comfort, fear, or pain. Even in moments where that connection did happen, they may have been founded in uncertainty about how long it might last and what might cause the next rejection.

| MELANIE |

My mother was not capable of regulating herself. She was in an almost constant state of fight or flight. For her, every day was a battle against imagined enemies. She was tortured by imaginary voices and real losses: like the loss of her marriage, the loss of her father, and the loss of her own mind. It's taken me until this period of my life to understand the very deep sadness that was always with her.

My mom exploded at us regularly. She chased us, beat us, dragged us, threw things at us, and screamed hostile words at us daily. And so, when I was angry, all I knew how to do was yell and run in circles. I knew no other way.

I may have been missing some important things in my childhood, but here's what I *did* have: a deep understanding of my feelings and a context for them. I had an ability to make friends and collect deep, meaningful relationships – perhaps not always the healthiest ones, but with loving people who took me as I was, stood by me, and usually made me laugh.

I had a desire to seek teachers and therapists to guide me. Somehow, I have always landed at the doorstep of amazing healers; I have an impeccable nose for great spiritual guides. These people saved my life, repeatedly. Although I actually felt stupid all through my childhood, I managed to discover in my young adulthood that I was smart and had something to offer: through the clarity that comes from experiencing so many life challenges, I could put myself in others' place. It's easy for me to empathize with others – to know exactly what they are feeling and what they need, whether they can express it to me or not. These messages have always seemed clear to me. Today, I can feel gratitude for this vigilance and intuition, because they have made me a better wife, mother, and friend.

Over the last several years, I have finally started to "mature my system." My reactivity has slowed way, *way* down, which gives me ample time to think and respond intelligently. Even when I can't or don't respond from this adult self, there's always this grown-up part of me saying, "Hold on, there! What's most important here? The correction or the connection?"

I'm doing what is required to heal the challenging outcomes of the disorganized attachment relationship I had with my mother, and I am breaking the cycle of reactivity with my children. If it's possible for me, it must be possible for anyone who dedicates him or herself to doing this work as a parent.

It probably comes as no surprise that disorganized attachment increases risk of some of the most common psychiatric diagnoses: ADHD, ODD, bipolar disorder, depression, anxiety. A strong link exists between disorganized attachment early in life and challenges in dealing with stress or a tendency to dissociate (to "leave" the situation at hand by mentally and emotionally checking out).

If, in your own childhood, you suffered abuse or neglect of some kind, you may have developed a disorganized attachment style. It would be expected that this would impact your own ability to form a healthy attachment with your child when you became a parent. Again – *this is not about fault or blame;* it is about recognizing that you may have formed 'default' ways of relating that are impacting your ability to manage your emotions and connect with your children the way you would want. Recognizing the impact of past upon present is a step toward changing how we define and experience ourselves in the present moment.

Human beings who are able to direct conscious attention toward their mental processes discover something surprising…it's not what happened in the past that creates our present misery but the way we have allowed past events to define how we see and experience ourselves in the present… The greatest damage done by neglect, trauma, or emotional loss is not the immediate pain they induce, but in the way a developing child will continue to interpret her world and her situation in it…We write the story of our future from narratives based on the past.

- Gabor Maté, *In the Realm of Hungry Ghosts,* p. 370

The good news is that as soon as you recognize and understand the source of your triggers, you can step into the present with tools that will eventually re-wire your defaults. You can reset to attunement; you can reset to steadiness, consistency, and even to the level of reflecting greatness. Every time you choose to go the route of the reset, this is what you are doing: re-training your brain. Know that you are living your greatness in every effort you make in this journey.

HOW WERE YOU ATTACHED?

The impacts of attachment on emotional intelligence and emotional management are created at such a young age that they feel natural to who the person is. Our purpose in outlining them here is to help create awareness of those defaults. Attachment style impacts our relationships by affecting how well we regulate, express, and manage emotions in ourselves, as well as how we connect with and attune to others.

Attachment relationships are also formed with caregivers other than the primary caregiver, and can be different from one another. A child might have a secure attachment to their mother and an insecure or disorganized attachment with their father, or vice versa. This is one of the reasons children do best when they have more than one caring adult to attach to.

The reality, for most, is a combination of these styles with different caregivers; and, for most of us, one is predominant. Quizzes about attachment styles are available online; find one if you are curious to find out your own predominant style. Most of us can guess what our own might be.

| LINDSEY |

My parents did their best to maintain a "normal" life with careers, family, friends and community involvement while dealing with my dad's quadriplegia, but they were under a great deal of strain. Most of the time they put on a brave face. But sometimes the pressure overwhelmed them and they descended into intense screaming matches. Although I was afraid of what they might say, I would hide under their bed to listen, to be close to what was happening. I was much more afraid of not knowing. I was terrified that my mom would get overwhelmed and leave my dad and me. The trauma of my dad's injury and the resulting separation from my parents when I was an infant left my nervous system on high alert for another possible disaster or abandonment. I remember having desperate thoughts about what I would do if I were left to take care of my dad on my own. Today, I know that my mom would never have left us; but back then, my childish interpretations made me fearful and drove me to try to keep the peace at all costs. It would have been unimaginable to me to knowingly do or say anything to upset my parents for fear of adding to the pressure cooker that was our home. I opted to be good. Compliant. Easy.

As soon as I was old enough to help, I was expected to assist my dad with daily tasks: eating, drinking, opening doors, turning the pages of a book, going to the bathroom. It was an uncomfortable reversal of roles. I was the caregiver and he was the dependent "child." This felt weird and wrong in a way that I never talked about. My parents, in their attempt to normalize our family life, didn't call attention to the strangeness of me caring for my own father's basic needs either. Because nobody said otherwise, I assumed that my resentment and embarrassment about taking care of my dad meant that I was selfish and uncaring. I did what I was told and did my best to hide my real feelings – which I thought I needed to hide to keep our family intact and functioning.

As a parent, I have noticed that I often want to sweep my own difficult feelings (or those of my kids) under the rug, the way I did when I was a child. It feels safer that way. But I know that it is healthier for my family to embrace a full range of experiences and emotions, so I am learning to express darker feelings, like anger, frustration, and disappointment in a straightforward and authentic manner, and to let my kids direct those same feelings toward me. It's still scary; I have a little girl's voice in my head that warns me of impending harm or abandonment. But I am trying to help that little girl inside me grow up, so I can help my kids grow up.

Consider: Were your parents reliable sources of comfort, support, and encouragement? Or did you feel as though the more difficult parts of you – specifically, your expressions of distress – were not welcomed? Did you feel suffocated, overprotected, or as though a parent needed you too much?

Were you allowed to express feelings – even those that were not so sweet and nice, like anger and fear?

When you were sad, did a parent talk to you, or were you told, "You have it so good – what do you have to be sad about?" When you cried, were you told to stop? Were your challenging emotions treated as a nuisance or as offensive by your parents? When you were afraid, were your parents dismissive, or did they tell that you were being silly?

Were you able to talk through discomfort, to face challenges and the tough emotions that come with them, and to come out the other side without being rescued by a parent who just wanted to make you feel better because of their own discomfort with emotions? Were all your emotions and true self honored and nourished, or was "being good" more about making sure that no one around you felt uncomfortable because of your intensity, needs, or big or challenging emotions?

Set aside time to write or talk to a trusted friend or loved one about this question of early childhood attachment and how this has impacted your relationships with yourself and those you care about. How has your parenting reflected these patterns? Do you see yourself as mostly secure, avoidant, ambivalent, or disorganized in your default ways of connecting with others? How does this show up in your life now? Honing in on your truth will open the door to a growing ability to reset. Perhaps more importantly, it will make it possible for you to convert your inner transparency into growth, empathy, self-appreciation, and greatness. This is how resetting can eventually bear the fruit of renewing – an evolution of the reset that will be described in more detail later on.

ATTACHMENT, VALIDATION, AND THE NURTURED HEART APPROACH

Insecure and disorganized attachments share a common thread: they both indicate a lack of *validation* of the child's emotions and internal experiences. *Psychology Today* describes validation as "the recognition and acceptance of another person's thoughts, feelings, sensations, and behaviors as understandable...a way of communicating that the relationship is important and solid even when you disagree on issues."[14] Validation is key to empathic connection and secure attachment, especially in those moments when the child needs a safe harbor for comfort and re-fueling. Being validated by caregivers is the way that children learn that what they feel, think, and do is OK. Through it, they learn to trust their own feelings, thoughts, and choices.

The Nurtured Heart Approach is, at its foundation, a profoundly

---

[14] https://www.psychologytoday.com/blog/pieces-mind/201204/understanding-validation-way-communicate-acceptance

validating approach for parenting and working with children. It offers a reliable formula for providing a safe harbor, encouraging exploration, and counteracting the effects of trauma on children and adults by creating ongoing healing experiences of healthy, uplifting connection. In using the Approach on yourself, you learn also to profoundly validate yourself. Each experience of validating your children and yourself will provide corrective experiences to over-write more negative internal programming.

In the next chapter, we will seek to understand how traumatic experiences in childhood can set certain "defaults" in the relationships we have throughout our lives. There is an overlap between the experiences described in this chapter and the one following; no one would rule out that some of what Michael, Melanie, and Lindsey experienced in their childhoods could be classified as trauma.

All this is offered in the spirit of recognizing patterns that we can choose to change.

CHAPTER FIVE

NURTURING HEARTS:
Healing Post-Traumatic Stress and Adverse Childhood Experiences (ACEs)

A traumatic event is one where a person feels triggered into fight-or-flight – where there is a perception of mortal danger – and neither fighting nor fleeing are options. Being in a car accident, having surgery under general anesthesia, seeing someone else violently harmed, witnessing a family member in the throes of addiction, suffering a severe injury or other accident, being severely ill, being a soldier in combat, witnessing screaming fights between family members, molestation or sexual abuse, or any other happenstance where a person feels trapped in a dangerous situation is considered traumatic. If that trauma is never acknowledged or the emotions surrounding it are never fully felt, accepted, or validated, it can leave a lasting pattern of reactivity that undermines our ability to manage our emotions.

Not everyone who has a traumatic event experiences post-traumatic stress disorder (PTSD), but this does not mean that these situations haven't had some important influence. The long-term impact of traumatic early experiences can be subtle. They can masquerade as mood disorders like depression and anxiety, as ADHD, or as challenges with executive function, healthy emotional expression, healthy relationships, or emotional management later in life. And an event does not have to be major to have an impact, especially for a highly sensitive person. Even seemingly minor disruptions in early childhood attachment can create challenges – disruptions like a few days of separation from the parent in very early life, or parents who were too preoccupied or stressed to closely attune with the child, possibly for very good reason – that then subsequently impact the child's reactivity and emotional health in adulthood and when they become a parent themselves.

It feels less blaming to point at mysterious biochemical factors, heredity, or environmental factors such as screen time as reasons why children are being diagnosed in record numbers with disorders like ADHD, ODD (Oppositional Defiant Disorder), Conduct Disorder, Intermittent Explosive Disorder, Substance Use Disorder, Bipolar Disorder, and Disruptive Mood Dysregulation Disorder. If we say that the behaviors that earn these diagnoses spring, at least in part, from disorganized attachment or early childhood trauma that could potentially have been prevented, it may seem to infer the holding of parents as responsible for these outcomes. This is especially hard to swallow when modern psychology offers so few ways to turn these issues around – and when standard care for mood and conduct disorders in children leans heavily toward medicating symptoms, sometimes for a lifetime.

Unless you grew up in an entirely nurturing home where your parents faced few distractions, obstacles, or intractable stresses, chances are that they faced some degree of limitation in delivering nourishing connection and relationship in your early life. To that degree there may be some lingering energies of developmental trauma that fall short of creating pathology, but that did have some influence. We bring this up to make the utility of the Nurtured Heart Approach – which focuses on restoration and renewal of the kind of nourishing relationship that builds healthy attachment and heals the sequelae of trauma – more easily understandable and clear. There is no blame. Most of us are doing the very best from wherever we are in our development, and with whatever we have in our repertoire of knowledge and possibilities. That said, the Nurtured Heart Approach has been instrumental for many in breaking cycles of limitation and making new vistas of human nurturance a reality.

Recent statistics suggest that one in every four children and adolescents have "one or more diagnosable mental disorders."[15] We don't want to resign ourselves to the idea that there is something wrong with

---

[15] http://www.merckmanuals.com/professional/pediatrics/mental-disorders-in-children-and-adolescents/overview-of-mental-disorders-in-children-and-adolescents

the brains of 25 percent of children and teens, nor do we ascribe to the medical approach when, in most cases, other avenues are available and effective. Interventions like mindfulness training, emotional regulation training, physical movement, creative expression, and EMDR (Eye Movement Desensitization and Reprocessing, which we'll cover later) are all promising avenues for healing what today is usually seen as something to medicate away. Nurtured Heart Approach practitioners have seen dramatic shifts in behaviors that elicit the diagnoses listed above.

The last chapter showed how some of the symptoms that lead to childhood mental health diagnoses could be an effect of early attachment; this one will look at the ways that adverse childhood experiences and childhood trauma could also contribute to difficulties with self-regulation, executive function, and emotional management in both children and the adults (and parents) they become.

DEVELOPMENTAL TRAUMA DISORDER:
THE DIAGNOSIS THAT WASN'T

In 2001, Bessel van der Kolk, MD, and Adam Cummings of the Nathan Cummings Foundation convened a think-tank to address the lack of an organization dedicated to studying the causes and effects of childhood trauma and to develop effective therapies where needed. They agreed that childhood trauma is "radically different from traumatic stress in fully formed adults"[16] and that it was probably behind many of the diagnoses being used to categorize children's most challenging behaviors. They saw a need for more research to discover whether psychiatry was misdiagnosing and improperly treating children who might share a common foundational problem of developmental trauma.

The team succeeded in working with Congress to create the National Child Traumatic Stress Network (NCTSN, http://www.nctsn.org) as part of the Children's Health Act. At this writing, there are 82 funded centers and 130 affiliate centers and individuals in 45 states and in Washington, D.C. Each site collaborates with local agencies,

---

[16] Van der Kolk, Bessel A., MD, The Body Keeps the Score: Brain, Mind, Body and the Healing of Trauma, Penguin Books, 2014: p. 157.

schools, hospitals, shelters, and juvenile justice programs. Through this network, van der Kolk's team surveyed the records of over 2,000 children and teens with multiple psychological diagnoses.

> *We soon confirmed what we had suspected: the vast majority came from extremely dysfunctional families. More than half had been emotionally abused and/or had a caregiver who was too impaired to care for their needs. Almost 50 percent had temporarily lost caregivers to jail, treatment programs, or military service and had been looked after by strangers, foster parents, or distant relatives. About half reported having witnessed domestic violence, and a quarter were also victims of sexual and/or physical abuse.*[17]

Of these children, 82 percent did not meet diagnostic criteria for PTSD – a disorder that is well understood and for which psychiatry has effective therapies. The stresses they have experienced are not so easy to pin down as a single traumatic event or situation. These children were in a kind of gray zone where they did not have standard PTSD symptoms. Instead, they seemed "shut down, suspicious, or aggressive" and tended to receive diagnoses like:

> *..."oppositional defiant disorder," meaning "This kid hates my guts and won't do anything I tell him to do," or "disruptive mood dysregulation disorder," meaning he has temper tantrums...Before they reach their twenties, many patients have been given four, five, six, or more of these impressive but meaningless labels. If they receive treatment at all, they get whatever is being promulgated as the method of management du jour: medications, behavioral modification, or exposure therapy. These rarely work and often cause more damage."* [18]

To address these issues, van der Kolk and 11 other researcher/clinicians spent four years drafting a proposal for a new category for the DSM-V (the updated version of the Diagnostic Statistical Manual, the diagnostic "bible" of psychology): Developmental Trauma Disorder. The diagnosis was built from consistent symptoms across 130 studies involving over 100,000 children and teens worldwide who had symptoms related to

---

[17] Van der Kolk, p. 158.
[18] Van der Kolk, p. 159.

abuse, neglect, trauma, or other kinds of harm during childhood:

> *(1) a pervasive pattern of dysregulation, (2) problems with attention and concentration, and (3) difficulties getting along with themselves and others. These children's moods and feelings rapidly shifted from one extreme to another – from temper tantrums and panic to detachment, flatness, and dissociation. When they got upset (which was much of the time), they could neither calm themselves down nor describe what they were feeling.[19]*

These symptoms were due not to genetics or brain dysfunction, but to minds, souls and bodies responding appropriately to lack of healthy attachment and to adverse experiences. As adults in their lives lacked tools to bring these young people back into a state of balance, distances would tend to grow and more difficult experiences would arise, compounding the initial problems.

Also common in the young people in these studies were disrupted sleep, physical symptoms like unexplained pain or sensitivity to touch or sound, self-harming behaviors, and issues with learning, language processing, and fine-motor coordination. Because it took so much energy just to maintain control over themselves, and because they were often in a state of fight-or-flight, these children were easily distracted and had trouble focusing on schoolwork and maintaining other aspects of executive function.

Dr. van der Kolk's team published articles on their findings, hoping they would be able to create a single diagnosis that would replace multiple ineffective labels. A team of mental health commissioners heard Dr. van der Kolk speak on this work at a national convening, and in response urged the American Psychological Association to add Developmental Trauma Disorder to the DSM and to prioritize related research.

Unfortunately, when the DSM-V came out in 2013, it contained several new diagnoses – including Disruptive Mood Dysregulation Disorder, Non-suicidal Self Injury Disorder, Dysregulated Social

---

[19] Van der Kolk, p. 159-60

Engagement Disorder, and Disruptive Impulse Control Disorder – but among them, Developmental Trauma Disorder was conspicuously absent. The DSM-V was widely panned as lacking scientific validity and reliability, and many experts stated that it wasn't an improvement over the DSM-IV. The British Psychological Society "complained to the APA that the sources of psychological suffering in the DSM-V were identified as 'located within individuals' and overlooked the 'undeniable social causation of many such problems."[20] Still, it was published on schedule, and every mental health practitioner had no choice but to purchase it, earning the APA upward of one hundred million dollars.

If DTD had been included in the DSM-V, what difference would it have made? Under the umbrella of a broad diagnosis that acknowledges the impact of parenting, preventive measures could be put in place. It would have helped highlight the importance of psycho-education and parent education through approaches like the NHA, where a simple set of behaviors and techniques helps adults regulate their emotions in ways that rebuild attunement and trust, giving children in their care an experience of being immensely valued, seen, and non-punitively held within a strong and loving set of boundaries. Work with youth across the entire spectrum of function and dysfunction has demonstrated that the healing impact of this approach is profound. Certainly, a child who is already experiencing the results of developmental trauma may require some therapeutic input to undo deeper damage, and having this diagnosis would help investigate and validate the impact of such therapies.

At the level of individual parents and children, this helps foster understanding of why resetting can feel out of reach for just about everyone, at least some of the time. Even in the best of circumstances, most parents face challenges that could impact their children's sense of security, leading to what might be a minor — but significant – developmental trauma. The Nurtured Heart Approach, through building attuned, consistently positive relationship, provides a simple and highly effective set of guidelines for addressing any level of

---

[20] Van der Kolk, p. 166-67

developmental trauma. There is no harm in implementing the NHA without a diagnostic category in place, with any child or any adult. It is a therapeutic process designed to help all children (and all adults) thrive when it is implemented with positive intention and consistency.

In service of deeper understanding of why resetting can be hard, and in service of holding awareness of what might be running the show inside the parents or children at a default level, let's look more deeply at the roles trauma and adverse childhood experiences might play in making resetting a challenge.

What We Know About ACEs (Adverse Childhood Experiences) and Lifelong Health

The Adverse Childhood Experiences Study (ACES) surveyed thousands of adults who were insured by Kaiser Permanente, and then tracked their health and well-being throughout the following decades. These researchers found that the number of adverse experiences a child has is a powerful predictor of mental and physical health across their whole lifetime.

Researchers developed seven categories of adverse experiences and mailed a questionnaire out to 13,934 adults who had already had a standard physical exam. The categories included childhood psychological, physical, or sexual abuse; violence against the mother; living with household members who were substance abusers, mentally ill, or suicidal; or living with household members who were ever imprisoned.

Those who responded received a score from 0-7. More than half of the respondents reported at least one childhood adverse experience; 1/4 reported more than two categories. Those who experienced four or more categories had a four to 12-fold increased risk of alcoholism, drug abuse, depression, and suicide attempts, and a two to four-fold increase in likelihood of being a smoker. Other factors much more common in people with four or more categories of adverse experience included a greater number of sex partners, poor self-ratings of health, sexually transmitted disease, physical inactivity and severe obesity. The more

---

[21] Van der Kolk, p. 166-67

adverse experiences people had, the higher their risk of heart disease, cancer, lung disease, bone fractures, and liver diseases.[21]

Early adverse experiences create long-lasting impact in our brains and bodies. Learning to manage emotions, identifying and de-fusing reactive triggers (Stand 1), engaging proactively in positive relationship with ourselves and others (Stand 2), and maintaining healthy boundaries and limits (Stand 3) are good for mind, body, spirit, and community.

Psychiatrist Gabor Maté, MD, quotes Eckhart Tolle in his book, *When the Body Says No: Exploring the Stress-Disease Connection* (Wiley, 2011): "Be at least as interested in your reactions as in the person or situation that triggers them." Maté advises us to cultivate "bare attention," where we can *notice* without reacting. The NHA takes this one step further: recognizing your own history of trauma or adverse childhood experiences gives you the space to notice their impact, and then – on a moment-by-moment basis – to work to reset to greatness around your triggers, using their energy to purposefully fire up next levels of greatness.

UNDERSTANDING TRAUMA AND PTSD

The first association many people make when they hear about PTSD is with soldiers returning from war. While veterans are at high risk, the consensus in the psychology and psychiatry communities is that 7-15% of people have experienced an event traumatic enough to develop PTSD. PTSD and disordered attachment may overlap: being abused by a parent is traumatic, and both disorganized attachment and traumas unrelated to parent-child attachment (being abused by someone who is not a primary caregiver, for example, or a bad accident, natural disaster, or death or illness of someone close to you) make emotional management harder.

A traumatic event is one where the urge to fight or flee is strong, but there is no escape. In people with post-traumatic stress disorder (PTSD),

---

[21] Felitti, Vincent J, et al. Relationship of Childhood Abuse and Household Dysfunction to Many of the Leading Causes of Death In Adults: the Adverse Childhood Experiences (ACE) Study. American Journal of Preventative Medicine, May 1998; 14(4): 245-58. Abstract online at http://www.ajpmonline.org/article/ S0749-3797(98)00017-8/abstract

a traumatic event has brought up the urge to fight or flee when neither is possible. Feeling helpless and stuck while also in grave danger has a long-lasting impact on brain and body, giving rise to PTSD symptoms: the re-experiencing of the event through flashbacks, nightmares, and other disturbing recollections; emotional numbness; a desire to avoid any place, person or activity reminiscent of the traumatic event; and challenges like difficulty sleeping or concentrating, feeling jumpy, or being easily irritated or angered.

PTSD causes people to feel defeated, dissociated, and depressed. People with PTSD also may harbor unexpressed rage that makes them fear that they might hurt someone else. They may feel shame, as though whatever happened to them was their own fault, or something they deserved.

Any discussion of childhood trauma and difficult childhood experiences can generate a sense of hopelessness or helplessness. It also, like attachment theory, can seem blaming of parents who are doing their best to do what might be the toughest, most exhausting job in the world. Again: we're all doing the best we can with the resources at our disposal. There is no blame here; only a journey to empowerment that comes from recognizing what might possibly impact your behavior and working to give yourself the freedom to choose differently in the present moment. The self-reset can be learned, no matter the gravity of the past; and this practice can be powerful medicine for change going forward.

'TOYS R US' AND TRAUMA

Parents who have come to the Nurtured Heart Approach to help a child who has experienced trauma have, at times, been stopped short by the Toys R Us analogy. Where there is a true, real, deep-rooted cause for a child's difficult behaviors, they reasoned, how can we ascribe those behaviors simply to 'energy-seeking'?

Advanced Trainer Nicole Semmens encountered this question from parents in a class she taught, and sought help via the NHA Advanced Trainers closed Facebook group. The responses she received from experts in childhood trauma were brilliant and helped many in the community see how important this approach can be in supporting these children.

Nicole posted a request: *Calling all ATs with experience working with trauma! I started a 4-week series last week and a couple of the participants were a bit triggered with the Toys R Us analogy. They didn't care for the "simplistic" idea that their kids with trauma were "just" trying to get their energy when there might be a deep-rooted issue/cause for the negative behaviors being exhibited.*

Psychotherapist and Advanced Trainer Elizabeth Sylvester: *I think NHA still applies in the case of trauma, but with a gentle shift. It is always appropriate to respond to a child's feelings – for example, "I see you are angry." Keeping energy low when a child is raging is especially important with traumatized children because excessive adult intensity is re-traumatizing (yelling, threatening). These children need a truly calm and unflappable adult so they can remain regulated and not be triggered. Also, if we focus on a traumatized child only when he is upset, or especially intimately when he is upset, we are reinforcing this as the child's most interesting identity. I think we need to strongly energize when the child is relaxed, having fun, and feeling joy to help the child recover a full, well-rounded identity, not just an identity based in having experienced trauma.*

Catherine Stafford, NHA educator, therapist, and author: *It's hard not to get tripped up by the language of that toy analogy. Don't let it throw you. For dysregulated children, regardless of why they have challenges with regulation, the idea that "we are the favorite toy" is not the most compassionate representation of our understanding of where the overwhelm comes from. I like to explain it as 'relationship-seeking' versus energy/attention seeking. You are radiating relationship and energy every moment; where is it flowing, and what are you celebrating energetically? This idea of relationship-seeking is active and intentional and keeps us focused on needing us to be fully present, attuned to the child's needs for support, being fully regulated/energetically congruent and co-regulating around the hardest of times. "You are your child's favorite toy," at first glance, implies an intentionality to behavior, but we need to remember that even kids who struggle with regulation notice how and when we show up.*

Nurtured Heart Approach trainer and peer leader, therapist, school special education administrator Veronica Coates: *I think the Toys R Us concept is relevant; it just may be for a different reason. For typical children who have not experienced trauma, their brains light up with the relationship with mom or dad any time. For youth who have experienced trauma (most likely multiple and ongoing traumas), their brains have literally rewired how they see the world and relationships. Oftentimes, healthy relationships are so foreign that they feel very uncomfortable there; youth in trauma want to escape that uncomfortable feeling of safety and healthy intimacy. So, instead of lighting up for the "toy" for the reasons of a typical child, youth who have experienced trauma may light up the "toy" to escape or seek a feeling of normalcy. This can look VERY intense, though, and outwardly appear as a 'behavior.' It could come out as aggression, taking off, or sexualized behavior...Their brains will (at times) try to recreate the chaos they are used to in order to help them feel calm. Teachers will often mistake these trauma-induced negative reactions as behaviors rather than reactions or reflection of having a traumatized brain. If traditional methods of discipline are used in these cases, they often backfire.*

There is a lot of research going on with complex trauma in children; all the interventions that are working dovetail with NHA (meet the youth where they're at, baby steps). With these youth, oftentimes, active recognition, just mirroring, or even sometimes just sitting parallel with them, drawing, being quiet are as much as they can tolerate.

Howard Glasser: *I might say that traumatized children have an even greater craving for connection, relationship, and healthy attachment. On their way to finding attachment based on aligned, healthy, loving interaction, their desperation to create this can make them more prone to seek alternative, negative ways to feel attached via a reactive interaction. Nurtured Heart is a way to heal this habitual mode of connection in real time, making space for the trauma to heal. The 'Toys R Us' metaphor is only a helpful way to understand the dilemma in present time, and an inspiring frame for standing fast in not feeding the energetic impression these children have acquired that negativity is the best route to creating and sustaining deep relationship. This simple analogy has given many people hope that they can move this mountain and restore the child to a positive way of being in the world. I know this to be true because so many children with histories of trauma have transformed the same intensity of suffering, anger and despair into manifestations of greatness.*

Consultant and NHA Advanced Trainer Toni Peck Rose: *The deep-rooted cause for the behavior doesn't change the fact that children still go for the fastest, easiest and juiciest connection – which, in most cases, is negative behavior or the relationship-seeking Catherine pointed out. NHA works beautifully with all children. The kids I've worked with who have severe trauma in their past thrive with its usage.*

RESILIENCY IN THE FACE OF TRAUMA:
ONE PSYCHOLOGIST'S STORY

Psychologist Peter Levine, in his book *In an Unspoken Voice: How the Body Releases Trauma and Restores Goodness* (North Atlantic Books, 2010), shares a story that illustrates how willingness to fully feel waves of emotion, along with warm support and positive acknowledgement, can heal the impact of trauma before it develops into a post-traumatic syndrome.

Dr. Levine is struck by a car in a crosswalk. As he lies on the ground waiting for the ambulance, a female pediatrician comes to sit beside him and offer help:

Her simple, kind face seems supportive and calmly concerned. She takes my hand in hers, and I squeeze it. She gently returns the gesture. As my eyes reach for hers, I feel a tear form. The delicate and strangely familiar scent of her perfume tells me that I am not alone. I feel emotionally held by her encouraging presence. A trembling wave of release moves through me, and I take my first deep breath. Then a jagged shudder of terror passes through my body. Tears are now streaming from my eyes…I am sucked down by a deep undertow of unfathomable regret. My body continues to shudder.

Levine goes on to describe in detail the waves of shuddering and trembling that wash over him in the aftermath of the accident, as well as emotions like fear, rage, and sadness. In the ambulance, he has an experience of wanting to move his left arm, and he lets the arm move where it wants to move – "toward the left side of my face – as though to protect it against a blow."

Suddenly, there passes before my eyes a fleeting image of the window of the beige car…I hear the momentary 'chinging' thud of my left shoulder shattering the windshield. Then, unexpectedly, an enveloping sense of relief floods over me. I feel myself coming back into my body. The electric buzzing has retreated…I have the deeply reassuring sense that I am no longer frozen, that time has started to move forward, that I am awakening from the nightmare.

He has a similar experience of remembering, in vivid detail, how he had protected his head by reaching one hand out to break his fall. As he grows calmer, he asks the paramedic to tell him what his vitals are. Since the initial moments when they had first measured his heart rate (170 beats per minute) Levine had calmed so much that it had fallen to 74 bpm.

I breathe a deep sigh of relief. "Thank you," I say, then add: "Thank God, I won't be getting PTSD."

"What do you mean?" she asks with genuine curiosity.

"Well, I mean that I probably won't be getting post-traumatic stress disorder." When she still looks perplexed, I explain how my shaking and following my self-protective responses had helped me to "reset" my nervous system and brought me back into my body.

"This way," I go on, "I am no longer in fight-or-flight mode."

"Hmm," she comments, "is that why accident victims sometimes struggle with us – are they still in fight-or-flight?"

"Yes, that's right."

"You know," she adds, "I've noticed that they often purposely stop people from shaking when we get them to the hospital. Sometimes they strap them down tight or give them a shot of Valium. Maybe that's not so good?"

"No, it's not," the teacher in me confirms. "It may give them temporary relief, but it just keeps them frozen and stuck."[22]

Levine shares this experience as a personal journey through Somatic Experiencing®, a method he developed to help people avoid or heal from PTSD. Where trauma is most harmful is in the ways it makes us feel helpless. Through paying close attention to physical sensations (like Levine's urge to move his left arm while in the ambulance, or the feeling in the other arm that led him to recall a way he protected himself during the accident), patients can "transform terrifying and overwhelming experiences."[23]

An animal who has just been chased by a predator and managed to escape will, like Dr. Levine after his accident, discharge the energy of

---

[22] Levine, Peter, In an Unspoken Voice: How the Body Releases Trauma and Restores Goodness. North Atlantic Books, 2010: p. 5-9.

[23] Levine, p. 10.

mortal terror by shaking and breathing deeply. Ann Marie Chaisson, a doctor of energy medicine who works as director of Andrew Weil, MD's integrative medicine program at the University of Arizona in Tucson, teaches people to shake in this way after they become emotionally flooded – a form of energy medicine that has been part of many ancient cultures. When humans do this in a setting where modern medicine is in charge, they are likely to be given drugs or tied down.

In the effort to return quickly to a sense of physiologic normalcy, we avoid giving over to the full sensations of and emotions about what has just happened. In trying to bypass these sensations and emotions, we fail to let our bodies respond as they naturally want to.

Fortunately, it's never too late to go through this kind of response. Levine reports that patients who are led through the Somatic Experiencing process shake and breathe deeply as they recover, even if years have passed since the traumatic incident. Becoming aware of events in the distant past that might have created unhealthy reactivity in the present; and deeply feeling, discharging, or transmuting the energy of the emotions stored up in the body around those events are foundations of the most effective interventions for people with histories of trauma or PTSD.

The synergy between Somatic Experiencing and NHA can be observed in the way Dr. Levine allowed and was supported in his natural response to the accident, and the way in which his emotions were felt as energies moving through the body. He had a calming, trustworthy person show up in a time where he most needed support; he listened to his body and attended to and allowed the energy of his strong emotions to move through it; and he celebrated his own resiliency after a traumatic experience. He experienced NHA on a cellular level, living out the greatness of an otherwise horrific incident by allowing his intuition and knowledge to guide him through.

Glasser describes the process of self-resetting out of a triggered moment using a term relayed by his colleague, therapist Dr. Elizabeth Sylvester: it is a sort of *metabolizing* of the energies impinging upon us, where we feel the truth of the emotions invoked arising in any moment, then purposefully metabolize those very energies to generate renewed messages to the far reaches of the body and beyond. Those same energies, he continues, can *metastasize*, getting 'stuck' at a cellular level and becoming so-called 'issues in the tissues,' if not welcomed in and actively renewed via what Glasser describes as a heart-centered greatness practice.

NO MATTER THE PAST, NURTURED HEART WILL HELP

Intention and attention exert real, physical effects on the brain.
- Schwartz & Begley, The Mind and the Brain, p. 289

If you, the reader, feel like a reactive mess sometimes, please know: *You can do this.* It just needs to be the most important thing to you. Ask yourself: is it more important that your child *[fill in the task or accomplishment or rule you want followed]* than have an intact relationship with you? Is it better in the end if your child finally obeys and does *[insert the thing you would give your left arm to have your child do on a regular basis without being nagged]*, or if you keep your respect for yourself, knowing that you've done everything you could to grow up your nervous system, and positively influence your child's, one response at a time? The irony is that the latter will likely lead to everything you had hoped for in the first place, and quicker than you might imagine.

Simply being able to say, "I'm feeling triggered/flooded right now, and I need to take a reset and calm and care for myself before trying to handle this issue with my kid," can make a big difference for the parent who is working to manage emotions in the face of unresolved developmental trauma.

If you feel at any level defensive or upset that your own unconscious patterning might have contributed to the issues you are experiencing with your child now, we understand. You might also feel resistant to acknowledging the impact of choices your own parents made when you were small, because you recognize that they were doing the best they could with the resources they possessed. **The assumption here is that we** *all* did the best we could with what we knew and what we experienced ourselves in childhood. This information is offered entirely in the spirit of awakening, healing, and creating more choice and power.

HEALING THROUGH THE NURTURED HEART APPROACH

Body and mind are deeply impacted – often, in ways that thrum below our conscious understanding — by traumatic experiences and disordered early attachments. Recognizing this, educating ourselves about where we might be stuck, and working to build emotional management skills will pave the way for inner peace, inner wealth, and healthy relationships.

The Nurtured Heart Approach is powerfully effective in every kind of parent-child relationship. It creates a consistent atmosphere of attunement, positive regard, and connected, loving, constructive ways of relating. The Nurtured Heart Approach works to build resiliency and executive function, both of which can be hampered by trauma or insecure/disorganized attachment. It captures and 'creates' a child in experience after experience of success at everyday tasks and in managing emotions. The lasting positive impact that has been anecdotally observed by NHA therapists and educators in highly intense and challenging children (and adults!) strongly suggests healing impact on the long-term consequences of difficult early childhood experiences.

Nurtured Heart parenting, when done consistently, will build inner wealth and the ability to manage emotions and live out greatness in children with all kinds of histories. It takes a present-moment approach to transforming intensity. No matter the history of the child with whom NHA is being practiced, its methods work the same magic: they help guide children to better self-control, self-respect, and self-love. They motivate children to use the inner strength they all possess to live out their greatness and to bond positively with adults.

No matter where you come from, if you can wholeheartedly commit to doing things per the guidelines offered here and in other resources on the Approach, you will move toward healing. Our nervous systems have the flexibility to change the default circuitry that comes from trauma or disorganized attachment.[24] In terms of the brain science of emotional management, the NHA is likely to work at many levels to heal the impacts of attachment issues and adverse experiences – to literally rewire the brain and create new defaults. As you learn and practice the approach – even if you struggle with it and make lots of mistakes, as we all have – you will be creating ongoing experiences of secure, loving attachment and safe, nourishing connection.

---

[24] Where PTSD is a factor, additional therapy might be helpful for discharging the impacts of trauma on the body that lie beneath conscious awareness. Van der Kolk and many others strongly recommend EMDR (Eye Movement Desensitization and Retraining), a therapy that focuses on the physical imprints of old traumas, allowing the person to briefly sit with the emotions they've been running from and 're-programming' the nervous system pathways that keep the traumatic memories activated and make emotional management hard. Author Melissa has had good experiences with resolving old patterns of emotional reactivity through this therapy. Peter Levine's Somatic Experiencing may also be helpful where unresolved trauma still inhabits the body.

CHAPTER SIX

YOU KNOW IT'S TIME
to Reset When...

In the next chapter, we'll look at 25 ways to reset ourselves. Some of them will be straightforward; others might seem to take a more circuitous route to the desired outcome. That outcome is that you are:

- Completely reset from giving energy to negativity (Stand 1).
- In your heart and feeling ready to unleash positivity (Stand 2).
- Poised to maintain and enhance clarity (Stand 3).

Our list of ways to reset is by no means comprehensive. It's meant to give you a diverse set of notions that will serve as a springboard for your own many-fold ways of resetting. It's also meant to help you see how much of what you already do can be characterized as resetting and cast intentionally in that light as you work the Nurtured Heart Approach.

Before we go there, let's review some of the ways you can know that it's time for a reset – where emotional floodwaters are rising or where a trigger is starting to take hold. You may, upon considering these, or over time, think up a few more that are specific to you.

CUES TO RESET

The practice of resetting allows you to be real about how you feel; to make use of the energy of all kinds of emotions and sensations; to avoid the unhealthy, counterproductive practice of stuffing challenging feelings when they seem inconvenient; and to cultivate the ability to attend to all emotional states with curiosity, fluidity and purpose.

The key here is *baby steps to awareness.* In the past, you might have expended enormous effort learning to suppress your emotions because that was how you survived a challenging childhood or period of adulthood (or both). Now you can inch your way toward greater awareness of your emotional state in each moment, and manage your expression of those emotions in ways that promotes your well-being and the well-being of your children.

Body signals/energy sensations in the body. While your mind may have no real idea that you're about to lose your cool, your body is incapable of lying. In the past, you may have been very good at pretending (to yourself and others) that you're "FINE!" when you really weren't – and you may have had a gold-medal-level ability to ignore your body's signals of distress. Recognize how powerful an ally this ability has been for you: what were you able to tolerate, move through, and even triumph over because you could do this? Knowing this, and holding gratitude for the way it has helped you in the past, begin to increase your capacity to pay respectful attention to your body's physical cues.

Remember the body signals you identified in Chapter Three: heart rate speeding up, face or hands turning hot, a twitch in the lip or eyelid, an urge to lash out physically or bolt from the room. As you build your awareness of messages from your body, you will get better and better at resetting before the flood.

Compulsive, self-harming, or addictive behaviors. Thinking that you *need* a drink or a sugary treat means it's time to reset. (Not that we are condemning alcohol or sugar; we just know that these pleasures can turn punishing and/or addicting when used to self-medicate.) Picking at cuticles or skin, overdoing it at the gym or failing to maintain a promise to yourself to exercise, or spending hours online without a purpose may also mean a reset is in order. The emergence of any addictive pattern suggests the same.

Always/never, blaming, gossiping, victim thinking. If you notice yourself saying to yourself or someone else: "He always...." "You never..." you're either on your way to a flood or already there. Always/never are never true, always untrue...when it comes to people's behavior. Reset.

If you notice yourself having blaming thoughts or speaking blaming words, it's time to reset. When you blame others, you place yourself in a disempowered position and place the other person in a position where they are likely to (1) play the victim; or (2) become defensive. It's a direction that is likely to lead to more negativity. Reset.

An urge to gossip – to speak negatively in a complaining way about someone who is not present – suggests that a reset may be in order. The moment you are thinking or complaining about being a victim of someone else's actions or words, it's time to reset. Victim thinking is the flip side of blame, but the two are equally disempowering.

Dwelling on, analyzing, or storytelling about something that has triggered you in the past; obsessively or repeatedly thinking about something that happened while looking for evidence that you were right and/or that your actions or statements were justified. This includes perseverating on anything you wanted to go differently or rehearsing repetitively things you wished you had said. Develop your ability to point out to yourself: "I'm in the past right now!" and to reset to what is going well in the present moment.

You recognize, in the moment, a trigger that you know is significant for you. Hopefully, reading this book has supported you in figuring out which triggers are most likely to sabotage you in maintaining the First Stand. These triggers tend to be associated with very early experiences and the early relational patterns you had with your caregivers. Make a list of your most potent triggers and commit it to memory. Practice noticing those triggers and resetting way before you lose your cool. Tell your loved ones about them so they can help you reset when you don't recognize them yourself.

Even if you are unaware of any emotions or physical sensations, and you *know* that something has been triggering to you in the past, there's no harm in taking a reset: "Oh, she's sulking. I know that this has been a big trigger in the past for me. I'm going to take a reset and find some greatness to acknowledge even though I'm not feeling particularly triggered in my body." Identifying and resetting in response to known triggers is a deeply compassionate path of self-inquiry.

─┤ **MELISSA AND WILLIAM** ├──────────────

We've been together as a couple since 2014. We have not fought much, but when we have, this has been our pattern:

1. Melissa says something that triggers Will.
2. Will feels a surge of emotion and adrenaline. He bolts to try to reset himself, but usually not before saying something angry.
3. Meanwhile, Melissa's trigger around feeling misunderstood is activated. She HAS to explain that he didn't interpret her statement properly and there's really no need for him to be upset at all. She's too wrapped up in her own trigger to see that the horse of Will's emotional flooding has already left the barn and stampeded down the hillside. She can go get in front of it (and get trampled) or she can give him a chance to cool off.
4. Usually, she can't resist getting a good trampling: Melissa's trigger around leaving something unresolved is strongly activated. If she doesn't reset, she gives in to the urge to chase Will and give him a hard time for running instead of staying in the conversation and talking it through.
5. The conversation turns into a battle between two people with no access to their higher thinking centers or their hearts. It takes hours, or even days, for things to return to normal.

Key to reducing stress and avoiding unnecessary conflict: to notice the triggers and reset instead of going with the skid. Each person in the dynamic is responsible for recognizing their own triggers and resetting. In the heat of the moment, it can be tempting to tell the other person about how important it is for *them* to reset right now, and why – but resetting works best when we choose it for ourselves.

CHAPTER SEVEN

TWENTY-FIVE
Self-Resets

We could list ten, 25, 100, or 1,000 ways to reset; the possibilities are endless. The key – no matter how you choose to reset – is to be emotionally regulated enough to DO it: to recognize when it's necessary by noticing a body sensation or impinging emotional state, or recognizing a situation that triggers you; and to choose at that moment, *before* you lose your cool, to re-engage your thinking, intentional brain, and to reset in whatever mode works best for you. Every time you go this route and regulate your nervous system, the brain pathways created by these choices are further reinforced, making the choice easier to access the next time.

Any time you attempt or accomplish any self-reset – those listed here, or any other – make a point of giving yourself energizing statements (Stand 2). The descriptions below of suggested resets contain language that we hope will help you in generating these energizing descriptions for yourself and in recognizing the good resetting choices of others around you.

No matter how far down the rabbit-hole you've gone, you can return to your NHA intentions and celebrate a successful reset. If you co-parent with someone who is on board with the Approach, you can help each other by suggesting a reset when you're too far gone to realize you need one, and vice versa. Soon enough, your children will be supporting you by giving these kinds of reminders, as well – if they haven't already!

I. Resetting with the Breath

The breath is always there: the body's automatic 'resetter.' Deep, slow, conscious breathing activates the parts of the nervous system that settle fight-or-flight and re-connect the higher brain with the limbic brain. As the reset becomes second nature, even a normal breath can provide a reset and a renewal to Stand 2.

A few options for resetting with the breath:

- Take one or two slow, deep breaths, taking care to exhale fully. Then, exhale a little extra to prevent hyperventilation and make room for the next inhalation.
- Count with the breath: down from eight for the inhalation, down from ten for the exhalation.
- Imagine your breath as a color or as light; picture it passing into your heart center (the very center of your chest). Imagine that color or light swelling inside your body as you breathe all the way in, and releasing out into the room as you breathe out.
- Breathe your triggered energy (frustration, anger, fear) into your heart; breathe out calm, peace, and gratitude. Try narrating it in your mind; for example, "I breathe in the triggered energies, trusting my heart to convert them to positivity; I breathe out greatness, as loving energy, to every cell of my body."
- Breathe into whatever part of your body feels the most tension; as you breathe in, imagine sending that energy into the center of your heart to be repurposed via Stand 2. Then, breathe this renewed, revitalized energy back out to the same parts of the body that initially felt tense, adding medicinal doses of appreciation.

CELESTE ELSEY, NHA TRAINER AND EDUCATOR

I have trained others in the Nurtured Heart Approach for almost a decade and created a Greatness Kids Initiative program in my home county to teach the Approach to students of all grade levels. I have had the honor of assisting Howard at the week-long Certification Training Intensives as a Peer Leader. At a recent training in New Jersey, I knew of some youth providers who were skeptical about the Approach for their teenaged students because they believed it was only suitable for young children.

When Howard leads these trainings, he takes the podium solo and teaches several hours' worth of segments on his own – an amazing feat of endurance and skill. The flow of each day's learning and the way each segment builds on the one before it is something that he tracks carefully and that has been created over years of refinement. If a question comes in that jumps too far ahead, he will always reset it and assure the person asking that the question will be answered later in the training. (At the trainings in New Jersey, Howie made the decision to let everyone know that he would not be taking questions during the week with the intention of supporting participants in answering their own questions; the results were fantastic.)

In the middle of a session at this training, I recognized a point in the learning curve where I could share a story to illustrate the impact of the NHA in older children. Eager to reassure the participants mentioned earlier, I raised my hand. Howard called on me, and I launched into the story. I wasn't quite done when I noticed him motioning to me to wrap up. I summed up in the closing sentence, and he stated, in front of 75 people, that I had taken my story too far for what he had planned for that morning, early in the week. He appeared frustrated at the disruption, but clearly got himself back on track with a solid reset.

I felt a hot surge of regret and embarrassment throughout my whole body. My mind was spinning with self-criticisms and defensiveness. And I had the special privilege of being seated where everyone in the room could see me, and where they had all heard me being publicly reset by Howard Glasser himself. They must have wondered what I would do next. Would I leave the room? Would I choose to stay feeling frustrated and ashamed? That's what I felt like doing. Fortunately, I've been doing this work long enough that I could stay where I was and reset myself. Part of my reset became self-talk focused on modeling a live reset for the group.

I felt all the energy of the emotions coursing through me while breathing deep and steady breaths. And I listened. Breathing deeply, I could remain open to what Howard was saying. All the noise in my head subsided. I heard him acknowledge the contribution I had made earlier and felt grateful.

At the break, Howard and I spoke immediately and he commented about how amazing I was to have reset so well and listened so deeply in the aftermath of something so upsetting. I congratulated him on his quick reset, and we both moved on cleanly with our connection intact.

2. PHYSICAL AWARENESS RESET

Simply notice how your body feels. Awaken to your senses. Feel your feet on the ground. Look around. Notice things in the room. Notice smells and sounds. Put your hands over your heart. Rub your palms together. Notice sensations on the surface of your body as well as internally.

Put words to what you see, sense, and feel. This brings the cerebral cortex – the thinking, rational, reasoning part of the brain – back online.

3. MOVEMENT RESETS

Take a walk. Run around the block. Kick-box with the couch. Do a few squats. How about some push-ups? Stretch all your limbs. Energetically shake your hands and arms. Shake your whole head and body, like a dog coming in from the rain. A mindful movement break involving yoga, walking meditation, or chi gong exercises might be most helpful for some people.

If you have time and space, reset frustrated or angry energy through a full workout. Intense exertion helps burn off adrenaline in your system. Even a few minutes of high-intensity physical activity can completely shift your energy.

4. RESETS IN THE BODY

Resetting can be as simple as a change in body posture or facial expression. The body and brain engage in constant feedback loops with one another. Just as the body's sensations and postures shift in response to our thoughts, our thoughts can be shifted through adopting specific body postures or facial expressions.

Researcher David Havas found that subjects couldn't generate feelings of anger while contracting muscles used for smiling (he had them hold a pen sideways in their teeth). When subjects held a pen in their lips to activate muscles used for frowning, they had trouble generating happy feelings.[25]

Notice how your emotional states translate to specific ways of sitting or standing or facial expressions. Experiment with altering these – taking a "power stance" as described in Amy Cuddy's research (page 63), cranking your frown into a smile, or otherwise changing your body posture to reset. This isn't just faking it until you make it – over time, as you consciously choose empowered, calm, happiness-inducing body postures and facial expressions, you will become more powerful, calm, and happy.

One study examined the impact of physical movement in unison on cooperation. Researchers put pairs of children next to each other on swings. Some were set swinging in opposition, while others were set swinging in unison. The pairs who had swung in unison were more cooperative in a task after they finished swinging than the pairs who had swung opposite each other. If you and another person are in a conflict,

---

[25] Havas, David A., et al. Cosmetic use of botulinum toxin-A affects processing of emotional language. Psychological Science 2010 Jul; 21(7):895-900.

try taking a quiet walk together and set your steps in unison; or – if you have a swing set nearby – replicate the experiment described here!

5. THE "PEACE PROCESS"

Coach Nicola Gordon teaches a technique she calls "the peace process," a body-centered way of attending to tough emotions. Rather than actively trying to change or shift the energy of the emotion in the body, she guides clients to (1) notice any uncomfortable parts of the body and identify the sensations felt there, and to then (2) send love to that exact spot in the body without trying to change anything about the sensations. "Imagine that this place in your body is a baby," she says, "and just send it lots and lots of love." As the client does this, the sensations morph and change; in a session, Gordon keeps dialoguing with the client to help them follow the sensations and continue to report on them.

In the context of resetting, one would simply notice the sensation, name it (silently or out loud), sit with it briefly (perhaps with a few deep breaths), send it love, and bear witness as the sensation shifts.

6. MUSICAL RESETS

Across cultures and centuries, music powerfully influences the way we feel and the level of arousal (fight or flight) we experience. The brain science behind the impact of music on our minds and emotions shows that it affects the more primitive parts of the brain, where reward, emotion and motivation are processed.

According to the research of neuroscientist and musician Daniel Levitin, PhD, music "improves health and well-being through the engagement of neurochemical systems for (i) reward, motivation, and pleasure; (ii) stress and arousal; (iii) immunity; and (iv) social affiliation." It is "one of a small set of human cultural universals evoking a wide range of emotions, from exhilaration to relaxation, joy to sadness, fear to comfort, and even combinations of these."[26]

| MELISSA |

I attended a five-day workshop on healing trauma at the Esalen Institute in early 2017 with psychiatrist and author Dr. Bessel van der Kolk and his wife, singer/songwriter Licia Sky. Dr. van der Kolk told a story about having gone to southeast Asia following the 2004 tsunami to help survivors who had been traumatized. When he arrived there, he saw survivors singing and dancing together, using music and rhythm to try to recover, and he noted how well they seemed to be doing with their own traditional ways of healing trauma and feeling connected to one another. Within a few days, however, Western psychologists had shown up, offering cognitive-behavioral therapy and psychiatric medication. "After Fukushima happened," he told our group, "I said to Licia, 'We'd better get over there before the CBT and Prozac people do!'"

Most people surveyed list emotional regulation and emotional impact as main reasons why they listen to music. Music directly affects levels of neurotransmitters, endorphins (natural opiates produced by the body), and hormones, bringing delicious feelings of chills or thrills down the spine, intense euphoria, or other kinds of pleasure. Keep a reset playlist handy on your mobile device.

Singing provides its own related benefits: deeply breathing to belt out a tune, releasing stored tension in the muscles, and creating a burst of endorphins and a hormone called *oxytocin* that reduces anxiety and creates feelings of pleasure and connectedness. Singers have lower levels of the stress hormone cortisol over time.[27] And (fortunately, for at least one author of this book!), you don't have to be a good singer to reap these benefits. If you need a reset, consider bursting into song; to raise your threshold for stress, join a choir or other singing group.

---

[26] Chanda, Mona Lisa, and Daniel J. Levitin. The neurochemistry of music: feature review. Trends in Cognitive Sciences, April 2013, Vol 17, No 4: 2013.

[27] http://ideas.time.com/2013/08/16/singing-changes-your-brain/

Dance, too, is beneficial to health, beyond its effects on physical fitness. If you need to reset, surprise family and friends by busting a move. Warning: this could lead to laughter, disbelief, or even an impromptu dance party on the spot. You may end up feeling much better, very quickly. If you believe that this is something you can handle, give it a try.

Beyond this, research shows dancing with other people, doing the same moves, has an immediate effect on pain threshold. Studies find that doing your own moves doesn't have the same impact, likely because this doesn't create the same endorphin rush.[28] Electric slide, anyone?

7. THE MINDFULNESS RESET

Jon Kabat-Zinn, MD defines mindfulness this way: "The awareness that arises through paying attention, on purpose, in the present moment, non-judgmentally, in the service of self-understanding and wisdom."

Pure mindfulness is about simply noticing what is, whether it's good, bad, or great. It is about developing the ability to tolerate whatever we might be feeling or experiencing. A mindfulness practice is something that brings us to a place of conscious awareness in the present moment, while acknowledging and accepting any feelings, sensations, or thoughts that arise while we attend to the present moment.

As soon as we add the intentions of the NHA, we move into more of a cognitive realm, where we impose mental processes to influence our present-moment experience. We are working to move the needle to a more positive space on the dial. Still: the reset itself can be boiled all the way down to simple mindfulness.

A mindfulness reset would involve shifting attention from whatever problem or challenge threatens our sense of calm to another present-moment experience. This can be done anywhere, at any time. Try:

- Taking a moment to sense completely into the taste and texture of food

---

[28] http://www.npr.org/2016/05/03/476559518/the-health-benefits-of-dancing-go-beyond-exercise-and-stress-reducer

- Looking around you, consciously noticing what you see, hear, and feel
- Washing a dish, paying close attention to all the sensory input you receive there: the feel of the water and sponge on your skin, the sound of the water in the drain, the solid feeling of your feet on the floor, your hipbones leaning into the sink

Most other kinds of resets can incorporate a mindfulness component. If you are a meditation 'newbie,' try one of the many meditation/mindfulness apps available online. Melanie especially likes Headspace. Podcasts and videos to guide you through meditations or mindfulness practices are also widely available online.

8. THE "NAME IT TO TAME IT" RESET

The simple act of identifying our own emotional states can reset us. Where reactivity rears its head, we can choose to pause ourselves and describe our emotional state rather than diving into reaction. Using greater detail and complexity in these descriptions – giving them greater *emotional granularity,* as psychologists would say – enhances the benefits of "naming it to tame it."

Greater precision, psychologists find, works to give you more material from which to construct your emotional states. The more variety and nuance in your descriptive language, the more varied and nuanced your emotional states become.

Research on this topic finds that people with more emotional granularity are less likely to lose it when they are angry or to self-medicate by over-consuming alcohol; they are more likely to see positive take-aways in the aftermath of challenging emotions; and they have better overall health (measured by number of doctor's visits and amount of medication taken) and emotional regulation skills.

In experiments, people high in granularity use a range of adjectives in reporting their experiences, while also describing the intensity of things like anger, embarrassment, guilt, and regret. People low in granularity will use angry, sad, or afraid to capture unpleasant things and excited, happy, or calm to describe pleasant things...the greater your granularity, the "more precisely" you experience yourself and your world. [29]

This is a form of Active Recognition that we can give to ourselves, and it activates our thinking brains, stimulating *metacognition* – a process of reflecting on our own thoughts, thought processes, and mental states. Through granularity, you are 'being' with yourself in a way that will feel internally successful. You are building both healthy perspective and inner wealth.

9. PARASYMPATHETIC NERVOUS SYSTEM ACTIVATION RESET

This encompasses many of the resets listed in this section. Anything that brings calm to body and mind will enhance the tone of the PNS, which will raise your flooding threshold over time. A few examples:

- **Deep breathing:** remember to make your exhalation a little longer than your inhalation.
- **Guided relaxation:** an exercise that engages your mind in relaxing your body in a series of steps: for example, imagining yourself lying on a warm beach, putting your attention on each part of your body, imagining warm sand flowing along each part as you focus on it. Take a class, purchase a book, or find one or more exercises that work for you through a Google search.
- **Yoga:** classes and a regular practice are great, but keep in mind that even a single yoga posture, with a few slow breaths, can reset you. Forward bending postures are calming. Try a forward fold: stand with feet hip-width apart, bend your knees slightly, and hang your upper body forward. Thread your hands into the folds of your opposite elbows and let your arms hang down. Bend your knees as much as necessary to feel relaxed in the posture – even if it means sitting down in a chair and folding forward onto your legs. Take several deep breaths in the pose; come out of it slowly.
- **Chi gong:** This is a form of meditative movement developed

---

[29] http://nymag.com/scienceofus/2016/06/people-with-high-emotional-granularity-are-better-at-being-feeling-things.html

in China over centuries. It is used to help balance and heal the body through specific 'forms' that can be learned from classes, in books, or on videos. Just as is the case with yoga, an ongoing practice is ideal, but even a single chi gong posture or movement will enhance parasympathetic nervous system activity and can be used to reset the body and mind. Paul Fraser is a chi gong master with whom Melissa has studied. Find his teachings online if you would like to learn about the practice: https://vimeo.com/channels/paulfraserqigong

- Moderate to intense exercise: a workout will initially increase sympathetic nervous system activity – raising heart rate and adrenaline – but afterward, you'll experience a rebound increase in PNS activity. Over time, physical conditioning will increase your PNS tone, so that your threshold for becoming flooded will rise.

10. CEREBRAL CORTEX ACTIVATION RESET

Any activity that engages the thinking, logical, consequence-recognizing part of your brain will help to re-activate the higher thinking centers and take you out of fight-or-flight. Try:

- Doing some mental math
- Saying the alphabet backward
- Writing down five words that begin with a specific letter of the alphabet
- Making up a limerick or haiku
- Solving a puzzle

11. MANTRA OR AFFIRMATION RESET

Mantras/affirmations are statements you say to yourself in moments where you need to give your thoughts a job while you pause and reset. Use the Stands or turn to a favorite brief quote or affirmation. Create inspiring affirmations that remind you of your highest intentions as a parent.

─ TAMMY JACOBS, NHA TRAINER ├─────────────────────

I have a few personal mantras (which I sometimes state internally, and sometimes out loud) that help me replace negative thoughts that come up when I feel I am not playing the game well:

1. I choose greatness...I am greatness.
2. My love cannot be depleted.
3. You don't get to choose how I love you.
4. The old me wants to give you some unsolicited advice right now, but I know you have the greatness of making wise choices and don't need it from me – so I am going to walk away and reset.

Write a list of these mantras; keep a few on deck. Perhaps you'll choose to write them on Post-it notes that you hang up around your home, at work, or in your car.

12. THE EMPATHY RESET

Another way to reset before the flood is through compassion and empathy. Buddhist teachings are a beautiful resource for figuring out how to be *with* others in their suffering instead of trying to shift it. This tactic is especially handy when a conflict or a stalemate between parent and child threatens to create flooding in the parent. Finding your way to a place of compassion for the person who is on your last nerve isn't easy, but it does impact the nervous system in ways that reduce the stress response.

Connecting with someone's suffering rather than resisting it might seem to go against the first stand. Keep in mind that it isn't about celebrating or creating drama centered on suffering, but about allowing and acknowledging – even privately celebrating – what is happening in the moment. As this happens, energy around suffering can be effortlessly redirected toward the positive. An empathic response makes the other person feel acknowledged about what they are feeling and paves the way for positive recognitions through that deepened connection. Seeking to be accepting and compassionate about your child's state of mind, desires, or emotions is a path directly back to your Stands.

On the other hand, it's easy to get drawn into – and drained by – a child's sadness, anger or fear as we attempt empathy and compassion. From the child's perspective, expressing these kinds of emotions can feel like go-to buttons to push to elicit powerful empathic connection. This can create an ongoing pattern where the child feels most seen when she's freaking out.

The adage about misery loving company? It's true. We all know that. Some of us are almost OK with being miserable if we manage to pull others into our misery with us! In the absence of connection around the positives of everyday life, this can feel like the surest path to intimacy.

It's important to recognize that your children, no matter what their age or developmental stage, are keenly attuned to the ways in which they pull your energy in and deepen connection with you. Gently withdrawing connection in moments where the child is melting down – and restoring it the instant you see the child moving away from dramatic expressions of negative emotion – is the most impactful and empathic strategy. A child who is having a hard time probably does not need rescue or even support in their fears or complaints. The all-important quality of resilience, the ability to bounce back in the face of challenges, will likely be better served by support around their courage to take the next step after a setback, and through reflecting the greatness inherent in those steps of renewal up to the present moment.

This level of empathy is attitudinal, not relational, so there is no active connection or flow of energy for negativity. It creates an internal compassionate space where you can appreciate the child for resetting and successfully handling whatever they were previously struggling with.

Reset to a place of compassion for *yourself* – using the Nurtured Heart techniques on yourself to recognize where you are being successful in the moment – when a child seems to be acting out emotionally: "Look at me! My kid is _____ and I haven't started yelling." The child sees you resetting yourself, and that example holds enormous energetic value for the child.

| MELANIE |

Lately, I have been reading and learning more about what compassion and empathy look like. A simple handout I read suggested that one way to regulate anger is to put yourself in the other's position and breathe from that place. If you can see where the other person is coming from – if you can have empathy – it's easier to stay regulated. I didn't realize that the next day after reading the article, I'd have an opportunity to test it.

My child was just getting over the flu. She was mostly better by the weekend, but it was hanging on a bit. Monday was a holiday at her school and one of her best friends had a slumber party on Sunday night. On Saturday, I let her know that I would allow her to go to the party and stay late, but I wasn't going to let her sleep over, because I knew she wasn't well enough to not sleep all night and then start school on Tuesday. She took it well, and we moved on. However, at 9 AM on Sunday, she began her campaign to get me to change my mind. We happened to be spending the day together, so there was lots of time together, in the car, in close quarters… lots of time for her to try every imaginable method — tears, logic, anger, sweetness – to dismantle my resolve.

Keeping this article in mind, I kept reflecting to her with honesty and empathy that I understood why she'd be so upset, and that I'd be upset too. I told her I felt what it would feel like to believe I was well and have something I wanted to do badly, and have someone tell me I wasn't well and I couldn't do this thing. I let myself really feel how hard that would be and expressed this to her. When she used anger, I stuck with it. "I'd hate me too if it were the other way around. I totally get it."

The point is, I never folded. I held on to two things I knew for sure: (1) her health would have regressed if I'd backed down; and (2) by backing down in that instance, I would be subjecting myself to more of the same strong-arming the next time she wanted to talk me out of a "no" answer. I recognized that the sooner she learned that NO meant NO and that her efforts wouldn't bear fruit, the sooner she'd quit trying. I recognized that all my folding in the past had given her the idea that if she continued this long enough, she'd wear me down, and I was completely committed that this wasn't going to happen.

I had told her that she could go back to the party in the morning and be with her friends if I could change a doctor's appointment I had scheduled for her for that time. While she was at the party, I received an e-mail from the doctor's office telling me the appointment could not be moved. I'm not going to lie to you—for a few minutes, I thought I'd rather pay for the missed appointment and let her skip the doctor. Instead, I took a deep breath and realized that this was my work. I texted that I was sorry, but she'd have to skip revisiting the party in the morning, and that I wanted her to know now. I made a conscious choice to not take the easy way out of a hard situation. To get to that point, I first had to be calm…had to breathe, to not act, but to give myself the space to become calm and think it through.

She was furious when I picked her up. She went to bed furious. I let her. I stayed mostly quiet and allowed her to be mad. When she talked to me rudely I reset her, but didn't shame her, and I energized her where I could. In the morning, she woke up kind, back to being her calm self. She didn't hold on to it. We ended up having a really nice day together. That night, she went to bed telling me what a great spring break she had with me, and how much she enjoyed all our hours together.

That day, I learned that one of the best ways to learn to stay calm, reset, and regulated is to take one thing from the arsenal and hold on to it. For me, on Sunday, that meant compassionately refusing to energize her negatively. In NHA terms, this was about Stand 1 *(Absolutely no! I refuse to energize negativity)* and Stand 3 *(Absolutely clear around rules and the giving of un-energized resets every time a rule is broken)*. And, while there are many subtleties that can be refined – like resetting her from all that perpetual insisting – at this moment in time, what was most important for me to work on with her was staying connected with her while holding the boundary. Consciously empathizing with her was key to meeting my goal of (1) not arguing or being critical of her and (2) continually energizing her.

13. THE "IS THIS REALLY AN EMERGENCY?" RESET

In a moment where you are about to fly off the handle because of a pet peeve, or because your child is having to be reset repeatedly and you're building a head of steam, ask yourself: "Is this really an emergency?"

No?

Feel that, fully. Recognize as many things as possible about this moment that *could* be emergencies, but aren't. Let that knowing return you to your Stands.

14. YELLING RESET

In certain moments, the buildup of energy and emotion can make it feel virtually impossible to speak in an even, calm tone. That's okay. Go ahead and yell – but yell energizing statements at your child. Yell them at yourself! This one works even if your initial intent was to launch into a disciplinary sermon.

---| MELISSA |---

I told my 13-year-old son to make his bed and put away his laundry. I went on my merry way, doing my own chores, and then found him sitting on the couch with his mobile device, YouTubing away. The bed was made, but the laundry was still on his dresser.

Angry, I launched: "NOAH! I...AM..."

Reset.

"...SO PLEASED THAT YOU WENT AND MADE YOUR BED RIGHT AWAY AS SOON AS I TOLD YOU TO DO IT!"

The look on his face was priceless.

"THAT SHOWS ME YOU RESPECT MY NEED TO HAVE A NEAT HOUSE AND MAKE SURE YOU DON'T CRAWL INTO BED WITH SPIDERS AT NIGHT!" Laughter. He put the phone down. He knew what was coming next. "Now I need you to..."

"Put away my laundry," he said. "Sorry."

"Thanks for being so responsive...this is the last time I'll bug you."

"You're not bugging me, Mom. Thanks for reminding me."

In another instance, I went to yell at my son, but then diverted into a self-reset: "I AM FEELING PRETTY FIERCE RIGHT NOW! I CLEARLY NEED TO TAKE A RESET! I AM RESETTING MYSELF! ISN'T IT GREAT THAT I KNOW TO DO THIS INSTEAD OF SAYING SOMETHING I WILL REGRET? IS THAT NOT THE GREATNESS OF DETERMINATION AND COMPASSION?" We all laughed and felt more connected.

15. THE GRIEVING RESET

Grief is a profound and sometimes crippling emotion that arises in response to loss. It can come with the death of a loved one, but it can also arise in less extreme circumstances: saying goodbye to some part of our lives we've grown used to, seeing an adored baby grow into a child and then into a teenager, or even for something going on in the larger world, such as climate change or a refugee crisis.

Whatever the source of grief, deeply feeling it and expressing it can feel almost unbearable, but it provides us with some of the most fertile "compost" for greatness. Some cultures encourage and embrace the full expression of grief; others suppress it or try to bypass it. Author Martin Prechtel, in his book *The Smell of Rain on Dust* (North Atlantic Books, 2015), writes that "Grief is praise…Grief expressed out loud, whether in or out of character, unchoreographed and honest…is in itself the greatest praise we could ever give…Grief is praise, because it is the natural way love honors what it misses."

Grief can show up in all kinds of ways – it doesn't have to be loud or demonstrative. It can be quiet and still. It tends to be all over the place over time. This is not about any one way of expressing it; it is about refusing to dismiss those feelings, calm them down, or ignore them to get on with our lives. In fully inhabiting our grief, we can find a deep reset to gratitude; even more, the depth of pain we feel in those moments can be a glimpse into its own kind of greatness.

MELANIE

In this last few years of her life, my mother has developed severe Alzheimer's disease. It has been both tragic and fascinating. As I watch her slip away, I find my way to new kinds of forgiveness. I enjoy just sitting with her. At last, it feels safe, because the dementia has taken over and is beautifully in the way of her schizophrenia. Of course, dementia is awful – but somehow, in this situation, I find it is simpler to understand and be with.

My therapist shared with me that this is not uncommon

for clients with mentally ill parents who develop Alzheimer's—the children are finally able to experience healing in the absence of the symptoms of the mental illness. This has been very true for me. Lately, every time I leave her, I cry in my car, grieving deeply for my mother for the first time. I grieve for what I will never have with her and how much I actually love her. The pain I feel is – and this is exactly the right word – *exquisite*. I have never felt it before. Each tear reconnects me, calms me, and shifts me toward more fluid emotional expression in the whole of my life. With each release through tears, I feel a deeper connection with my mother's truest self... the person she would have been without her disease. I feel myself strengthen by being able to feel all that love. And, I feel grateful to experience that love while she is alive and while I can express it back to her. This is the greatness my grief has brought me—a true, deep healing.

16. THE ANCIENT HISTORY RESET

In this reset, we use all the good work we've done to recognize how our own "buttons" – those installed very early in our own lives – came to be; and to reset in moments when those buttons are being pushed. To continue to recognize where ancient history is compelling you to reactivity, ask yourself, in a moment when you feel that body clue, and sense that the flood is coming, "When have I felt this way outside of my life as a parent? Before I had children?"

| LINDSEY |

My teenage daughter and I started watching a particular TV show as a way of spending special time together. One night, I was tired and couldn't keep my eyes open. I went to bed and she went on to watch the next episode without me.

Although part of my brain remained aware that it was only an episode of a TV show, my emotional reaction to this "rejection" was huge. I felt a very old feeling of abandonment. Still, I was able to slow down, consider my interpretation of what was happening, and connect what I felt to experiences from long before I had kids. Of course, it wasn't my daughter who was causing me hurt in the present moment; her behavior was just a trigger. To find my way back to this wisdom, I went from the body sensations (nausea, terror) to a place where I had the thoughts on deck. Because I could accept fully where I was in that moment, I could recapture my perspective and cleanly reset, even amid uncomfortable feelings. I could remember that it isn't what the other person is doing that makes me safe or unsafe; it's the old stories that bubble up inside of me.

17. THE COMPOSTING RESET

Howard Glasser sometimes likens the resetting process to composting: the transformation of waste into nourishing food. Redirecting energy and nutrients from wastes provides new crops packed with good nutrition.

In a 2013 article in *National Geographic*, writer Brian Clark Howard describes New York City's ambitious plan "to increase composting of food scraps generated by the city's eight million inhabitants." Instead of burying 1.2 million tons of food waste in landfills each year – costing $80 per ton – mayor Michael Bloomberg sought to employ the services of a local composting plant to turn all that food waste into nourishing compost. He also proposed a plan to "hire a company to build a plant that will turn food waste into biogas – methane that can be burned to generate electricity just like natural gas."[30]

The metaphor, we hope, is clear. If we see crises, challenges, problems, or other sources of negativity as compostable resources, we can see how much pure energy they contain – energy that can go directly into growing the most nutrient-dense greatness imaginable. From wastes, we

---

[30] http://news.nationalgeographic.com/news/2013/06/130618-food-waste-composting-nyc-san-francisco/

can grow food, or we can produce clean, limitless, pure energy. We get to decide what kind of composting we'll do, moment by moment.

Consider yourself to be a highly advanced composting device, capable of turning virtually any kind of waste into pure greatness-growing energy. Create a written or visual meditation on composting to greatness.

Begin to think of this energy as something that has substance and mass. It can accumulate over time if not consciously worked with, discharged, and redirected. In this story from Melanie, she recalls how she learned this: in one moment, we think we are fine, and then some small thought or occurrence tips the balance and the flood comes in fast.

MELANIE

A couple of years ago, the kids, Joel, and I went on a hike. One of my kids complained the whole time, feeling very afraid of snakes and bugs. She was anxious, and her intensity was spilling over. I imagined that her "container" was inadequate to hold her big feelings, and the job I gave myself was to hold her feelings in *my* container and show her how to manage herself.

I could do this for a while. I tuned in to how she was feeling and took it all on. I energized her as much as I could. Nothing I tried calmed her down, but really, it was fine – or so I wanted to convince myself. We were on a trail loop, and we were already too far to make turning around a feasible solution for ending her (my) discomfort faster. We had to just let her go on about it and keep hiking.

After about 20 minutes, my heart began to beat faster. My anxiety began to rise. I was feeling my own "container" filling up and overflowing with her powerful expressions of emotion. Because we were on a hike, it was easy to walk ahead of her and reset, so, overall, I thought I was keeping my cool because I was patient and not seeming reactive. But that wasn't necessarily the case.

Right after the hike, we went to lunch. We were having a nice time laughing together. But I caught myself thinking, "How long will this last?" Within minutes, as though on cue, the girls started fighting; and boom, I felt overwhelmed, and I was unable to manage my emotions. My over-filled "container" blew a big old hole.

In retrospect, I see that when energy begins to flood – even if it's just trickles, to begin with – I might think, "Good. I'm in control here. I am not yelling. I am okay," but the truth is that the energy is stored in the body. A person who is naturally reactive, like me, needs to become aware of this and dispense/disperse that energy in an ongoing way...which is what I *didn't* do on the hike. It wasn't enough for me to just hold it all in my body. Doing that meant setting myself up for overflowing into a flood when the next challenging moment arose.

I got an intimate look at my own reactivity on that hike. I got to see a process that usually happens too fast for me to track: the movement toward flooding from telling myself that *everything is fine* when what's really needed is a quality reset (or 10); the holding on to the irritation; and, eventually, the irresponsible release of the stored feelings. When a fight happened, I wasn't prepared to handle it responsibly and gracefully. Another teaching moment for me: as the energy builds, it must be composted to greatness through conscious self-resets.

18. CREATIVITY RESET

Creative expression is a form of composting to greatness. From the raw energy of emotion, we can choose to make something: a drawing, a poem, a dance, a piece of music. In modern Western cultures, it is easy to fall into the belief that art is only for people with talent or artistic skill; but for most of human history, forms of creative expression have been woven into everyday life. In a recent review published in the

American Journal of Public Health, the rationale for this is made clear:

> *...There is evidence that engagement with artistic activities, either as an observer of the creative efforts of others or as an initiator of one's own creative efforts, can enhance one's moods, emotions, and other psychological states as well as have a salient impact on important physiological parameters...Over the past decade, health psychologists have cautiously begun looking at how the arts might be used in a variety of ways to heal emotional injuries, increase understanding of oneself and others, develop a capacity for self-reflection, reduce symptoms, and alter behaviors and thinking patterns.[33]*

Studies of sand play, dance movement therapy, drama therapy, music, expressive writing, storytelling, drawing, and mandala making show that creative expression reduces stress, improves coping ability, and speeds healing from illness. It reduces depression and anxiety, reduces cortisol levels, and boosts mood.

Even if you have never felt yourself to possess artistic talent, choose at least one artistic modality with which you feel comfortable, or about which you have some curiosity. Keep a paper journal and colored pencils handy for moments where challenging emotions start to bubble over. Keep a sand tray or modeling clay in your office or home. Begin to consider these kinds of expression when resets are warranted. Be purposeful in bringing the energies you're resetting into your heart; then, re-purpose them – send them out to all your cells and beyond into your chosen expressive medium.

19. ACCEPTANCE RESETS, A.K.A.
THE STOP ARGUING WITH REALITY RESET

Acceptance looks like a passive state, but in reality it brings something entirely new into this world. That peace, a subtle energy vibration, is consciousness. – Eckhart Tolle

---

[31] https://www.ncbi.nlm.nih.gov/pmc/articles/PMC2804629/

The possibility of acceptance lies just beneath the surface of any moment where you feel most like fighting. To accept means, most simply, to choose not to do battle with the reality that lies before us, even if that reality is one we wish did not exist. Howard Glasser likes to point out that we are always choosing whether to celebrate the current reality; that we are, in fact, "never not choosing." Recognizing this makes it easier to embrace the perspective that the current reality is always shot through with greatness worth celebrating – all we have to do is remember that we have the choice to see things this way. It does not mean defeat; it is, in fact, the beginning of true agency. If we insist on doing battle with what cannot change, we cannot put our energies into creating what we want.

VIOLET

Organization and follow-through are among my son's greatest challenges. He leaves a trail of clothes, homework papers, personal items, used Q-tips, and electronics wherever he goes. Expensive jackets, hats, and sweatshirts go missing because he takes them off out in the world, drops them, and forgets to retrieve them. He feels awful about it every time, but this has not changed his pattern.

Caring parent figures have strived to get him to be more aware and organized since he was small, and it has never made much difference. Recently, I realized that a lot of my frustration about this has come from my holding a belief that he should be different. He should be able to learn this skill of tracking his stuff. He *should* try harder. He *should* prioritize this.

What's true is that right now, he simply does not seem to have this gear. Expecting him to have it is like expecting the baby first learning to walk to run the 100-meter hurdles. It leads to more frustration for me and less inner wealth for him. It instills in him a sense of failure, even if I don't explicitly criticize him for falling short of my expectations. On the other hand, if I accept that this is just the way it is right now – this is my kid and this is one of the things he does – I can relax and get back to my three Stands. I can generate true appreciation where he seems to be building better organizational skills in the smallest of ways.

If he develops good organizational skills, it will be because he is motivated to develop them in the way that works for him – not because adults around him are telling him he *should,* but because it matters to him. I can help create this by energizing any movement toward better organization, by acknowledging him for every homework paper slid into the folder and every day he gets himself ready and out the door on time with all the moving parts he must track to do this. All these moving parts reveal my son's greatness of determined effort; of thoughtfulness; of responsibility and respect for himself and others.

The acceptance reset might go something like this: "This is how my child is." (Bring in several second-stand acknowledgements of what is going well for the child, or that is not going wrong.) "I reset myself from any belief that he should be different." Or, "My expectations are running the show. I reset myself to the greatness I see in this moment," and list some qualities you see.

20. IMAGERY RESETS

In the early 20th century, a group of movement researchers developed a practice called *ideokinesis,* which uses guided imagery and metaphors to help improve posture, movement ability, and movement fluency. The science behind this practice demonstrates that mental imagery can have immediate effects in the body. Guided visualizations and other mental practices designed to heal the body further support the notion that we can reset the body in a real, concrete way with the mind.

To support a deep energetic reset, develop a few images you can visualize that represent the reset for you, and bring one of them into your mind's eye when a reset is called for. A few we've heard:

- Unplugging the toaster
- Snipping the wires to the energy source
- Hiding the buttons
- Being made of Teflon (or your other non-stick coating of choice; negativity slides right off)
- Water off a duck's back
- Burying the hatchet

21. CLEANING RESETS

One of Melanie's favorites! If you feel the flood coming, start cleaning. Do so mindfully, focusing your senses on the task at hand. As long as you aren't using toxic chemicals, take deep breaths, too.

22. HUMOR RESETS

Bringing lightness and humor to a triggering situation alters the physiology of everyone involved, fast. It should go without saying that sarcastic humor or other humor intended to bring others down will feed negativity and defeat your purpose.

LINDSEY

One afternoon, my then 14-year old daughter was playing the piano. I went to sit next to her on the piano bench, and she surprised me by literally jumping up and running away, screaming, "You touched me!"

As you know about me by now, feeling separate from and rejected by my children is one of my main triggers. This could have wrecked me, but instead, I chose to reset. "Oh, my gosh!" I yelled back, in my best melodramatic voice. "I am so sorry! I can't *believe* I did that!" I went on in this same faux-horrified vein until we both collapsed in laughter.

Humor and laughter are harder to access for some of us than for others. We encourage you to actively explore developing your range of humor and your willingness to reset into laughter when you feel triggered. Remember: all emotions are energy, and you get to choose how you move them through you and how they are expressed. In general, try to have at least one good belly laugh a day. With YouTube, Facebook, and other social media sources, finding something funny is easier than it's ever been.

23. REFLECTIVE LISTENING RESETS

Reflective listening is a communication practice that involves two steps: first, holding the intention to listen deeply and understand what the speaker is trying to communicate; and second, to offer verbal confirmation that the speaker's words have been heard correctly. It is a process where the listener pays respectful attention to the other person's words, letting go of any kind of response or retort and focusing completely on ensuring that the person speaking feels heard and understood.

This is a powerful practice in and of itself – and hard to master in the thick of a conflicted or triggering moment. It can, however, be just the thing to restore a sense of calm and connection when tempers are flaring. In the heat of the moment, it can be helpful to remember that in reflecting what you have heard, you are not necessarily agreeing with, or endorsing, what the speaker has said. Really, reflective listening is a form of Active Recognition: a direct acknowledgement of what the person is saying, without value judgment or reactivity.

The process is simple: listen intently, then say back to the speaker what you heard them say: "I heard you say that…" It's important to phrase it this way, in case what you thought you heard isn't what the person thinks they said. You can check in after you reflect: "Did I hear you right?" That's it. Once you have fully heard the other person, they may be more ready to hear your experience. They may be even more responsive if you add a related recognition of greatness at the end of the reflection; but this practice works on its own as an Active Recognition.

When an escalation threatens, reflective listening slows everything down. If you can remember yourself enough to take a reflective listening reset, it will activate your higher brain functions and give the other person time and space to calm out of a flooded state as well.

24. THE PIE (PHYSICAL, INTELLECTUAL, EMOTIONAL) CHECK-IN RESET

Another way to reset yourself is to take oncoming triggers or body signals as cues to engage in a structured check-in with yourself. One such check-in follows a PIE structure: how am I doing physically, intellectually, and emotionally in this moment? Use an Active Recognition foundation here, but also allow yourself to give yourself other kinds of recognitions as you move through the check-in. This can be written down, spoken aloud, or thought internally. This is a self-inventory—not something to do with the child, if you are in a triggering moment with that child. The Nurtured Heart Approach asks that we withhold from the child that their negative choices can get a rise from us. Still, this kind of internal check-in can be done during a reset with another adult or internally without anyone else knowing.

Physically: What sensations do you feel in your body? ("I feel a buzzy heavy feeling in my chest. My legs feel restless.")

Intellectually: What thoughts do you notice? Is your mind racing? What stories are you telling yourself? ("I notice my mind is busy with thoughts that my daughter might be lying to me right now. I appreciate myself for not just accusing her, but taking time to reset before I say anything else.")

Emotionally: What emotions are predominant? ("I feel fear and anger.")

Then, feel the emotions fully, and work to compost or otherwise move their energy to Second Stand acknowledgements as you renew into the next moments. ("Right now, I am actually handling my strong feelings amazingly well. That is great control and empowerment.")

25. THE TAPPING RESET

EMDR, which we mentioned earlier in this book as a modality for healing the impacts of trauma, involves thinking or talking about a triggering event while holding two small vibrating devices, one in each hand. They vibrate one at a time, alternating left and right in a regular rhythm, delivering bilateral stimulation (visual, auditory, or tactile stimuli that occur in a rhythmic left-right pattern). As the person recounts the event and holds these small devices, their nervous system is led to respond differently to the trigger than it has in the past. Something about the new input from the back-and-forth vibration helps re-program the person's response. The physical fight-or-flight reaction is uncoupled from the thoughts of the event.

Bilateral stimulation creates relaxation and less "stuck-ness" in your thinking, so that whatever has been bothering you is easier to let go. It has a distancing effect from problems and reduces worry. You don't need EMDR devices to create bilateral stimulation; you can do "butterfly taps" (cross your arms and tap one bicep with one hand, then the other bicep with the other hand), alternating taps of your hands on your thighs, move your gaze from left to right in a regular rhythm, or alternate tapping of your feet on the floor. This is a great, subtle way to take a reset and a wonderful trick to teach children as you help them learn to reset themselves.

Many forms of tapping, also known as "emotional freedom therapy" or EFT, have been developed. Some involve tapping acupuncture points on the body. Visit http://www.thetappingsolution.com to learn more. All varieties of tapping help to reset the physical stress response.

The next level for the tapping reset incorporates something called resourcing, where you envision a time where you felt soothed, inspired, or some other positive state, or envision a comforting, protective figure. In your mind, go to your greatness place while tapping to cultivate a sense of safety and peace.

Resetting to Greatness

Any of these resets can be "notched up" through what Howard Glasser calls "greatness practice," an internal application of the Nurtured Heart Approach with which he has experimented for several years. This practice entails taking the energy of WMDs (worries, misery, doubts) and any other impinging energies and 'resourcing' it by moving it through the powerful heart center and pouring that very energy back into inner claims of greatness. For example: in a moment of feeling unsafe or unsettled, he might internally breathe all of the energy he can access into his heart and state, as he breathes it back out, "I am the greatness of safety and peace." In a moment of feeling as though he may not be able to accomplish a goal, he might say to himself, "I am the greatness of action and accomplishment."

As you develop your own strategies for resetting, consider how you might integrate this notion of moving the clogged-up, fragmented energy of negativity through your heart space, transforming it into renewed energies of greatness.

Howard's book, *Igniting Greatness,* focuses specifically on this practice, which is a form of self-coaching that ties beautifully into the self-coaching practice described in the next chapter of this book.

All Resets are Self-Resets

This brings us to a crucial distinction – or, more precisely, *lack* of distinction – between resetting ourselves and resetting children or other "others."

Although we have addressed these as separate entities, calling them First-Stand and Third-Stand resets, there's some basic truth to the idea that **all resets are self-resets.**

The child who achieves a successful reset has ultimately reset himself. The adult who is reset by another adult (as in Celeste's story from the CTI training with Howard) is resetting herself. When a caregiver initiates a third-stand reset with a child, it is not a command, nor it is it a punishment: it is an invitation. It is a gentle reminder that a line has been crossed – whether a universally ascribed-to line (no hitting!) or one that is specific to one person's boundaries or preferences (such as the line Celeste crossed in the training with Howard). One can interpret such a reminder as an affront or attempt to be over-controlling; but there is immense power in receiving the invitation not as a slap, but as an opportunity to pause and consider what one is doing, and to then make a conscious, non-reactive choice about how to proceed in the interaction. There is never any harm in taking that pause and moment of reflection, even if ultimately it turns out that no line has really been crossed at all. We are always going to reset eventually, so why not do it sooner than later?

When that invitation is heard non-defensively and accepted, it is a cause for celebration, every time. The child or adult who resets is recognizing their own power and choice in creating the life they want and the person they wish to be, moment to moment. This is one of the many ways in which establishing a family culture where resetting is supported has enormous benefit.

With this in mind, let's move on to the final piece of the self-resetting picture: a personal practice called Appreciative Self-Coaching, developed by Howard Glasser with a small team of Advanced Trainers over the year or so during which this book was being written. This practice can be seen as a radical notching-up of the self-reset. We invite you to try it on and see where it takes you.

CHAPTER EIGHT

NOTCHING UP THE SELF-RESET:

Howard Glasser on Greatness Practice and
Appreciative Self-Coaching

As the creator of the Nurtured Heart Approach, I want to thank you deeply for going on this journey with Melanie, Lindsey, and Melissa. It's my belief that every parent – really, every *person* – who comes around to this Approach with openness and curiosity, and who decides to apply it to themselves and in their relationships, helps make a more peaceful, loving, positive world. This work is my greatest passion and it continues to be endlessly gratifying. Thank you for taking part in a movement that has grown a great deal since its earliest years and continues to grow.

I feel excited and proud of the ways in which this book adds to the body of knowledge and practices that are the most current evolution of the Nurtured Heart Approach. And there's been a personal benefit for me as well: in learning about emotional management and the impacts of developmental trauma, I have felt some old material bubbling up, waving an internal flag, vying to be reconsidered in my greatness journey.

One of my personal and ancestral realms of residual and unresolved energies is in the realm of family trauma. I find that working with energies that impact me in the present – resetting around current happenings – occasionally brings up 'historic files' of similar energies from the past: stories that have been energetically stored in the tissues of my body. Metabolizing these energies in the present creates opportunities to move them into renewal and into the light of greatness.

In this chapter, I want to share about my own journey of resetting, self-appreciation, and renewal through greatness practice and appreciative self-coaching:

- The greatness practice is an inner form of the Nurtured Heart Approach that has helped me become ever more mindful of my purpose and ever more able to take advantage of the energy of conflicting thoughts, feelings and situations that bump me offline. The more I funnel my energies into growing and living greatness, the quicker I recognize when I am offline (to my greatness) and the more empowered I am in my ability to not only reset, but to *renew* to an ever-more notched-up level of greatness. After years of practicing this, it has become evident to me that if I can move the needle on the greatness I am propelling, every aspect of living reverberates and reflects that growth in positive manifestations of what I have chosen to nourish.

- Appreciative Coaching has enabled me to begin to codify this practice and teach it to others.

I find that both the inner and outer use of the Nurtured Heart Approach continually evolve and expand to meet the needs of those who are learning and applying it. You might say that this chapter presents the 2.0 version of the self-reset: the advanced version, something to experiment with and make your own.

It is undoubtedly a significant and transformative step to be able to harness our energy and return from a reactive state to a more neutral, non-reactive one, especially under challenging circumstances. Excitingly, as I've pursued this work, I have come to realize that there is even more potential to be manifested from redirecting those energies. Once I realized that I don't have to just return to the status quo via a reset, I felt how I could actually catapult to a whole other level of *renewing*. Renewing describes a way of arriving at an entirely new place through transforming energies and making them purposeful and useful. I've been endlessly fascinated with exploring the possibilities of resetting and renewing, and an entirely new level of being alive has unfolded for me.

SELF-RESET 2.0

A reset is an act of love. One resets when they are honest enough within themselves to be able to lovingly be in the truth of anything that brings up strong emotions or any other thoughts or energies that are impinging on the present moment. It's a way of being impeccable. A reset can be as simple as an imperceptible pause or a single breath – after all, our bodies naturally reset by way of the breath, until the day we die; breath serves that purpose, whether we are mindful of this ongoing reset or not.

When I recognize that I need to reset – which I might do hundreds of times in a day! – I move through the same process you have learned, adding my own particularities:

- I consider the energies impacting me due to factors in life, love, or politics – those of anger or frustration, most often, but the energies in question might also be sweet and blissful.
- Right away, I acknowledge that I will use those energies to renew – that I will refuse to allow them to *metastasize* in their current form, but will instead transform and *metabolize* them.
- Negative energies are generally considered to be undesirable. Those who do not recognize them as potentially transformative or who have not yet gained the skills to manage their power will often want to slough them off, bypass them, or sweep them under the rug. These are the very energies I refuse to let run through my fingers. Instead, I use them intentionally and purposefully for propulsion.
- The farther offline I've gone, the more I can be aware of the need to reset; and the more I've become aware of greatness, the more I can be aware of when I've gone offline.
- When processing reset energies in the present, I listen internally for signs of whatever greatness will serve this opportunity going forward. Sometimes the trail of breadcrumbs quickly leads to an inner knowing of what greatness will be just the right *medicine* – just the right antidote in this and similar situations. Sometimes that greatness flashes as bright and large as a billboard; sometimes I need to intuit, experiment

and explore to find it.

- I then 'compost' or channel that energy through the heart, then using those same converted energies to nurture new or existing realms of greatness.

- Imagery can be used powerfully to move 'issues in the tissues'—where negative energies can become lodged—into the resetting process. While we can certainly reset only in our heads, the shift is exponentially more powerful when it includes the whole body. One example I have been playing with a lot recently: I imagine drinking in whatever fragmented, residual and unresolved energies are impacting me through a trillion straws that extend from my heart into every cell. I then imagine sending this renewed, clarified and *lightened* energy back out to every cell and beyond, knowing that it now contains perfect primal nutrition for the journey forward into greatness. With this practice, I send medicinal messages of greatness to every nook and cranny of my being and out into my world.

NURTURED HEART APPRECIATIVE COACHING

Appreciative Coaching is a structured way for adults using the NHA to support one another in "baby-stepping" to next levels of success in using this approach with youth. As the name suggests, it does not follow the typical coaching framework of "observe, critique, advise." It accomplishes its aims by providing only intentional and potent appreciation. This process is taught to Nurtured Heart Approach Advanced Trainer candidates at week-long Certification Training Intensives (CTIs) to help prepare them to coach those to whom they teach the NHA in a way that is completely aligned with the Three Stands.

Coaching without "constructive criticism" or advice? Yes. By bringing out the person's own wisdom and greatness through a gradual deepening of recognition, appreciative coaching activates the solutions that person is most likely to be able to actualize – the steps that, when gifted with awareness, begin to appear on every next horizon. The appreciative process itself progressively reveals to the recipient their greatness and evidence of those next steps inherent in their unfolding greatness.

Practice using this model in retrospect, first, to celebrate successful resets or energizing moments you've had that day. Over time you will learn to incorporate it on the fly as you work the Approach or any other aspect of your life. Rather than allowing your moments of success to pass by unacknowledged, use this practice *internally* to re-parent, re-fuel and renew yourself.

Appreciative Self-Coaching centers upon:

- Journeying with yourself as an appreciative witness to your own process
- Journeying into being the hero of your own story – discovering and owning your greatness
- Creating space for any new iterations of success into which you can unfold and blossom

This coaching model uses intentional self-appreciation as a vehicle for "baby-stepping" to next levels of success and for cementing and accelerating progress made by way of nurturing your own heart.

NURTURED HEART APPROACH APPRECIATIVE SELF-COACHING: WRITING/SHARING EXERCISE

Take out your journal or sit down with a trusted friend or co-parent. Then, move into these five steps.

IMPORTANT!

Between steps, pause and breathe deeply into what you are recognizing. Feel the movement of energy within your body and the enlivening of your heart. This step – the breath – is as important a part of this process as any other part, so please don't leave it out! Give your heart a voice to speak its appreciative truth.

With my Peer Leader team, I developed a series of steps for Appreciative Self-Coaching that can be remembered using the acronym SARAH:

WHAT I **S**EE, FEEL, HEAR, SENSE IS...

WHAT I **A**PPRECIATE ABOUT THAT IS...

WHAT THAT **R**EVEALS TO ME IS...

I **A**M/YOU ARE...

BREATHE THIS INTO YOUR **H**EART

S

...WHAT I SEE/FEEL/HEAR/SENSE IS...

Think of the last especially challenging moment in which you reset successfully. Feel into the emotions you felt as you encountered the situation and reset. If there are any details to remember about how you went about the actual reset, recall those as well. Remember the situation in your mind, heart, and body.

Consider, in detail, how you successfully used the Nurtured Heart tools to deal with the triggering situation. How did you engage Stand 1? Stand 2? Stand 3? Once you have considered all these aspects, take a moment to simply breathe into the feeling of recognizing this. Slow down. Give your heart a voice.

Pause. Let your heart speak. Breathe.

A

...WHAT I APPRECIATE ABOUT THAT IS...

Reward yourself with Stand 2 appreciations. Acknowledge yourself for being able to identify whatever triggered you, and to recognize your own responses/reactions as they came up. Use language rich with detail – remember the importance of *emotional granularity*. Remember to energize yourself for the greatness of what *did not* happen (what could have been "not-great") as well as for what *did* happen.

Pause. Let your heart speak. Breathe.

R

...WHAT THAT REVEALS TO ME IS...

Deepen: What do these choices reveal about you? Your qualities of greatness? Allow yourself to look at these qualities in detail. Expand upon each quality as much as you can.

Pause. Let your heart speak. Breathe.

A

I AM/YOU ARE...

Continue to name and breathe into the qualities of greatness you are recognizing in yourself. Feel them as your own, as a gift to others, and as a limitless shared resource.

Pause. Let your heart speak. Breathe.

H

...BREATHE THIS INTO YOUR HEART.

Take even more time, now, to sit with what you have recognized and breathe it more deeply into your heart. Imagine breathing all the greatness you are claiming back out to every cell of your body/being and beyond.

Any time you find yourself falling into storytelling, problem-solving, or negativity during this process, reset yourself back to the simple deepening of acknowledgment. Acknowledge concerns that arise as reflecting discernment – your attraction to problem-solving as reflective of your desire to move forward.

If any of your thoughts or feelings contradict your self-appreciation or owning of your greatness, feel the energies surrounding that and use those very energies to own your greatness at an even greater level.

Engage in Appreciative Self-Coaching at least once a day; bedtime or first thing in the morning are good times. Some people do this throughout the day. I personally would love to wake up one day and find this process to be my new default setting.

Write out your self-coaching sessions until you can run smoothly through the steps in your mind. Eventually it will be second nature and you will be able to resource these on the fly.

Here is an example of how this might play out in a self-coaching session:

S (See/Sense): *I resisted giving energy to the negativity that I noticed when my child was about to break our no-arguing rule. I gave him a recognition for his restraint when it looked like he might break the rule, but hadn't. I felt myself getting frustrated. I kept my cool, reset myself, and was able to hold off until I could see him being successful. Then, when he did break the rule, I felt that body signal of my heart racing and my face getting hot. I felt fear and anger. I still managed to give him an unceremonious reset and got right back to appreciation.*

A (What I Appreciate): *My sense of timing was right on. I adhered to the stands of the approach. I stayed wonderfully present and my appreciations of him were genuine and authentic. I expressed compassion for him and I stayed in my heart. I used my strong feelings to up my greatness of resolve. I truly appreciate all of this.*

R (What that Reveals): *This reveals that I have the greatness of discipline and of compassion. I also have the greatness of presence and emotional control. It reveals that my hard work to learn and implement the NHA is paying off. It's becoming clear and second nature for me.*

A (I Am…giving and owning greatness): *I am the greatness of discipline. I am the greatness of compassion. I am the greatness of presence and emotional control.*

The final step **(H – breathe this into your heart)** happens in silence; energy cultivated through the emotions and reset is actively moved throughout and beyond the body with the breath.

Owning greatness can be challenging. Again, if at any point your mind begins to interrupt or contradict you, practice a reset, breathe, and come back owning your greatness even stronger. If you find yourself becoming frustrated, channel the energy of frustration into deepening your sense of nurturing your great qualities – the growing constellation of greatness that is you.

I recognize that the process I describe here is completely outside of the norm of the way people ordinarily communicate with others and with themselves. If the language and Stands of the Nurtured Heart Approach as used in parenting seem weird and out-of-the-box, this is even more so! That said, I and others I've taught this to have found that if we can talk to ourselves in this way – even a little bit – it gives us a direct experience of self-talk that is in total integrity at the soul level. It removes all the self-critical subterfuge and gives us a direct experience of a profound level of self-appreciation. The models offered here are only suggestions; even if one does some part of this, not perfectly according to the script, that is quite okay! I know from my own experience both the giving and receiving of anything that at least matches this model in spirit stops me in my tracks, makes my day, and feels revitalizing.

SAMPLE SARAHS

Just as with the Stands and techniques of the Nurtured Heart Approach, this SARAH self-appreciation technique may at first feel like a clunky step-by-step. Over time, you'll make it your own. Here are examples from Melissa, Melanie, Lindsey, and Howard of recent SARAH self-coaching sessions:

MELISSA

One of my pet peeves with my house full of teenagers is when they cook food and leave a mess in the kitchen, then spread out around the house to stare at their electronic devices before cleaning up. Not diving into harsh lecture and punishment mode often requires a serious reset on my part before I open my mouth. Once I get through my own reset, reset the kids, and have them come back to do their clean-up, I can run through an appreciative self-coaching moment like this one:

S (See/Sense): *I saw the mess in the kitchen. And I refused to bark at or lecture the kids about it. They needed a reset too and I waited to give it to them until I could do it calmly and directly, with eye contact and a gentle but firm tone of voice. My face got hot, my heart beat fast, and I got hyper-focused on every little crumb and dirty dish in the kitchen, and I still didn't blow up.*

A (What I Appreciate): *I didn't let my desire to always be in control of my surroundings make me say mean things to others. I appreciate about myself how I always assume everyone's doing their best, and they are coming around to wanting to be more helpful instead of resenting my reminder to clean up after themselves. This speaks to my greatness of compassion and generosity. Gradually this way of working on this problem is bearing fruit – as long as I stick with the Stands, I continue to see growth and I feel as close as ever to my teen kids.*

R (What that Reveals): *This reveals that I have the greatness of patience and of letting go of a need to be a control freak – which is SO deeply ingrained in me! It reveals how much I love and care for my kids – that I want to support them in developing a sense of responsibility for the collective rather than doing things just because they're afraid of making me mad or having a consequence. I believe this is how to instill healthy, balanced self-care habits for the rest of their lives. This resetting in the face of a huge trigger is challenging, and I'm not afraid of a challenge!*

A (I Am…giving and owning greatness): *I am the greatness of love, patience, and generosity. I am the greatness of giving others the benefit of believing they are doing their best and want to be helpful and supportive to others.*

The final step (H – breathe this into your heart): My favorite piece: a moment to breathe and be still in the moments following a successful reset, renewal and reconnection with my kids.

| MELANIE |

One of the hardest moments in our parenting-filled week is getting the kids out the door on time for the long drive to join our carpool and to school. I have tried many, many things; more times than not, my kids move too slowly, oblivious to the stress and strain both parents are feeling. Few things give me a more immediate sense of anxiety than knowing people are waiting for me. I can sense their judgment and annoyance. On a day when this happened, and I didn't lose my cool, I tried a SARAH afterwards.

S (See/Sense): *The difference I could see today – on a day that was just like most, where the kids were moving like molasses to get ready to leave – was me. I was absolutely resolute that no matter what, I would remain calm. I had no desire to feel crazed to be on time. I was not willing to drive a little faster. I was absolutely not willing to start lecturing my kids, making them responsible for how I was feeling. I stayed utterly calm the entire time. I had relaxed shoulders and drove peacefully. I let my kids know why being on time helps us stay safe, and discussed ways to leave earlier – but I completely resisted lecturing.*

A (what I Appreciate): *I appreciate that I didn't let my anxiety take over. I appreciate that I stayed calm and loving. I appreciate knowing that I can only control myself, not anyone else. If they're late, they're late, and they will have to endure the consequences from school or irritated friends in a carpool. I appreciate how much my kids and I enjoyed the ride together. When they left the car, both looked at me and told me they loved me. If I had been upset with them, I would have only seen the back of their heads as they walked away. I appreciate that because I stayed calm, no repairs were necessary.*

R (What That Reveals): *This experience reveals my strength. I was not willing to sell my kids out by making a carpool's wait of a couple minutes more important than our peace of mind. It takes some serious inner strength to opt for my children over managing what others think of us. I showed that I understand that I am the only one I can control. This takes hard-core self-regulation. The way we were together reveals how much we enjoy being together and how much we love each other.*

A (I am): *I am the greatness of being strong and independent. I have learned to be self-regulated – which, to me, is the highest and deepest compliment I can pay myself. Because I am self-regulated, I am a safe person to be with. In having the greatness that is self-regulation, I show my kids that all my emotions are an invitation for an enriching life.*

H (breathing into my Heart): I breathe in the pride of being strong and emotionally regulated. I breathe in the love I have for myself and let that radiate to every part of me. It extends all the way deep inside of me and flows outside of myself, all the way to my children.

HOWARD

A handful of times each year, I teach the Nurtured Heart Approach at a week-long certification training that is intended to take treatment professionals, educators, and parents on a journey of learning NHA deeply and using it profoundly. It prepares them to officially teach the approach as well.

One requirement for attending this training is having had some kind of introduction to the approach – a one-day seminar, for example, or an online course, or having applied the approach after reading one of the other NHA books. Over the years, we have done everything we can to ensure that no one shows up at a training under duress – because they have to be there, as opposed to choosing to be there. As foolproof as we try to make those safeguards, once in a while we get wind that someone has been sent by his or her agency as a last-minute, unprepared replacement for someone who couldn't make it. Sometimes, an agency or district will send someone who is essentially braced against NHA to try to get them to come around. In both these circumstances, I feel strong concern that hold-backs and naïve participants will cause those who are there 'on purpose' to be inhibited from diving deep, unobstructed.

On the day a training was to launch, I found out that such a person would be in attendance. I immediately felt surges of anger, fear, resentment and dread. It hit hard and caught me off guard. I was so feeling like indulging my reactivity. It was right there, like an old friend, despite my having strived all these years to essentially change my default setting to being fully positive. There it was…and there I was, leaking negativity and on the verge of going way beyond just a small leak.

More often than not, these days, I can catch the hint of these varied kinds of surges and take advantage of the energy. I can usually drink it in and use it constructively. But this one? It took many resets – a series, really – and a truly concerted effort to channel that intensity into graciousness and understanding. Once that transpired, I found my way to the gift of Self-Appreciative Coaching:

S: *What I saw/experienced was that I quickly felt overwhelmed with strong feelings and a desire for things to be different than they were.*

A: *I appreciate that I gave myself the gift of transparency and of feeling these powerful feelings. I appreciate that I didn't slough them off – or, worse, pretend they weren't happening. I appreciate that I had the presence of mind to reset as many times as needed, and to know that I wanted to take advantage of all this intensity to grow my greatness even though it felt like it was out of reach.*

R: *What that reveals to me is my undying perseverance and my undying belief that energies of all kinds can be*

*breathed into this heart – this heart that has, after all,
handled everything up to now, and that can be converted
to everything I want to nurture, mindfully and consciously.*

A: *I am the greatness of undying perseverance, undying
belief, mindfulness and consciousness. I am that greatness.*

H: Breathing into my heart.

LINDSEY

My three kids were all born within a period of a little
over three years. David and I went from being a couple to
being a basketball team. I have loved watching the way
my kids' proximity in age has lent itself to closeness and
an ability to share interests, activities and even friends. As
the mom of 3 very small children, I felt needed and loved
and at the center of their tiny universe. Of course, it was
challenging to deal with all their diapers and strollers
and car seats all at once, but even in those early years, I
knew that those "little kid" challenges would likely pale
in comparison to the challenge of having three teenagers
at once.

At the writing of this book, my kids are 17, 15, and 14.
I am fascinated by the adolescent phase. I absolutely love
getting to know the interesting and multi-dimensional
human beings my kids are becoming…and it is most
definitely a challenging time as well. As I have described
in other chapters of this book, one of my primary reactive
triggers is feeling separated or disconnected from my
kids. As teenagers, all three of my kids' brains now have
a biological mandate to create separation from me. My
challenge, then, is to reset whenever my reactions to
their separation tempt me to try to interfere with this
necessary and healthy process.

S: *I see that when my teenagers push away from me,
I can stay conscious that it is a healthy and normal part*

of their development. I feel my own anxiety come up, yet I have the awareness not to blame my kids for how I feel.

A: *I appreciate that I have the discipline to pause during a reactive moment and take care of my own feelings. I appreciate that I don't expect my kids to curtail their development in order to accommodate my worries.*

R: *My ability to pause and reframe reveals to me that I have inherent strength and wisdom to draw upon when parenting gets difficult. I am able to prioritize my kids' healthy development over my fearful need to keep them close.*

A: *I am the greatness of my commitment to my evolution and that of my entire family.*

H: I breathe into my heart a love for my children and myself that is free of co-dependence.

SARAH 2.0

Jessica[32], A Certification Training Intensive alumna, shared with Howard about her use of the Appreciative Self-Coaching during the period it took to move through a difficult transition from victim of marital abuse to strong, independent, confident and self-loving single parent.

S: *I see a woman who has a huge capacity to love, who can continue loving someone when most other people would have stopped a long time ago. I see a woman who is no longer in a destructive relationship. Breathe.*

A: *I appreciate the fear you feel: the fear of being alone, the fear of being unlovable and unworthy of love because you can never be good enough, the fear of hurting people you love, the fear of not being able to cope. The fear of aggression. The fear of crisis. I appreciate that after years of being 'beaten up,' followed by years of beating yourself up, you have nurtured yourself and have come to a place*

---

[32] Names and details have been altered to protect this contributor.

of deep knowing that you have greatness and even that it has been there throughout. The debilitating sense of shame is easing. Breathe.

R: *This reveals to me a woman with a huge heart and a deep sensitivity to others' feelings, wanting to put others before herself. This reveals to me a woman who is healing. Breathe.*

A: *You are the greatness of compassion. You are the greatness of resilience. You are the greatness of being kind to yourself.*

H: Breathe. Cry. Tears stream down your face and won't stop…Breathe.

She wrote to Howard: "The greatness I unexpectedly discover in the SARAHs I write floats towards me like a life belt when I feel I am drowning. I have a 31-page document full of SARAHs written in those drowning moments. They heal me."

CHAPTER NINE

CONCLUDING THOUGHTS

on the Power of Resetting

Resetting is truly an act of love. It is an act of giving: either as a gift of clarity for another that a line has been crossed, or as a gift of clarity for oneself that crossing a line is something you personally are not choosing.

For a period of a few years early in his career, Howard worked with families who had their children removed by Child Protective Services and who, despite efforts to reunite, stood in the real possibility of having parental rights permanently severed. What stands out in his memory is how often those parents would say the actual words "I love you" during supervised visits, while decidedly not doing what was necessary to put love into action – to treat love not as a noun, but as a verb.

This was true even after Howard would tell them, as their court-assigned therapist, that he could go to bat for them if they put into motion the approach to parenting that he knew to be a better fit for their intense child. Some of these parents would rise to the occasion and bring all three Stands into play; others were too entrenched in relating to their child through negativity.

This didn't mean that these parents did not love their child, or even that they did not try to live out that love in the way they had been conditioned to expect love to show up. The result, however, was a continuation of the kind of blow-ups that had led to court involvement in the first place. "I love you" was sincere, but it wasn't enough to shift the relationship dynamics in a way that could reunite the child and parents.

Willingness to recognize a need for guidance to be the best parent one can be: that's love in action. So is the willingness to seek out that guidance, discern which is best, and implement it. Willingness to remember one's intention to parent with integrity and purpose on a difficult day? Definitely an act of love. So: in showing up to read this book, reading this far, and working to implement what it recommends, you are *being love.*

Giving oneself the gift of honesty in sensing the wave of 'triggered' feelings that are happening, and realizing that you don't want to be reactive, is a much greater act of love than pretending those strong feelings aren't happening.

Giving oneself the gift of feeling those strong emotions in honesty opens the door to the gift of using that energy to engender clarity (Stand 3) and the gift of not giving that energy to negativity – but, rather, pouring it into growing further greatness (Stands 1 and 2). Those are acts of love.

Choosing to not act out the triggered energy, and instead choosing to consciously use the greatness of empowerment and self-control to mindfully refuse to give relationship to negativity, are acts of love.

Choosing to sit in clarity around what comprises negativity, perceiving this through your own nuanced sensitivities, observations and perceptions; being that true to your own true nature, that true and aligned with what is right for you: this is an act of love as well.

How *not great* would it be if you ignored lines crossed for the sake of pleasing others or due to insecurities? So: how *great* is it that you honor your true self and hold others and yourself in accountability? That, too, is an act of love.

Giving and taking resets, holding Stands 1 and 3 to create the space for Stand 2 – this is unobstructed love. This is the energy of "I love you" taking form as a flow of gratitude, appreciation, and recognition.

Loving practice of Stands 1 and 3 leads eventually to more space where resets are unnecessary; and where love flows without impediment. In light of resets being fully established, ready and waiting as needed, Stand 2 can flow abundantly, expressing love and greatness.

And, as you hopefully have discovered: love IS the answer.

ACKNOWLEDGEMENTS

MELANIE GRETSCH

Thank you to the open and profound heart of Howard Glasser. I cannot think of another person on earth who would take a conversation led by two fans of his work and tell them to go write a book about it! His generosity and brilliance are what make NHA so utterly transformative.

Thank you to Melissa Lowenstein, who led the journey with so much ease and love. With her immense talents and incredible knowledge for Howard's work, she guided us on this prodigious journey.

Thank you to Lindsey Strasberg, whose friendship makes this whole parenting thing just a little bit easier. Her support and acceptance are life-altering. Best friends forever.

Thank you to my children. Their love and their protests have made me stronger and deeper. Being their mother has taught me to love and forgive myself. These two are my spirit guides. I cherish every single minute of parenting them.

Thank you to my husband. Love of my life. We are on this journey together, hand in hand, for the long haul.

Last but not least, thank you to my parents. My relationship with my mother may have been difficult, but I owe her everything. I will forever treasure her. And my father has always been my rock—the one constant source. I love him with all my heart.

LINDSEY STRASBERG

Thank you, Howard Glasser, for creating the wonderful world of Nurtured Heart and for trusting us to explore its contours and add our voices. Thank you, Melissa Lowenstein, for being the backbone of this process. Without your intelligence, passion and commitment, this book would not exist. Thank you, Melanie Gretsch, for your tremendous wisdom and your impeccable instincts for finding the best teachers. My life is so much better for having you in it! And, finally, thank you to the members of my family who let me publicly delve into some of our most difficult moments and allowed me to reveal how wonderful and wonderfully human they are.

MELISSA LOWENSTEIN

Thank you to Howard Glasser for believing in this idea and for doing so much to bring it fruition. Thank you to Melanie and Lindsey for being a dream-team of collaborators—you both have incredible heart and depth, and it's been an honor to share in this journey with you. Thanks to my work family at AHA! in Santa Barbara for supporting me in continuing to follow my passion for writing and for the Nurtured Heart Approach. Much appreciation also to the far-flung NHA tribe, many of whom provided feedback, stories, and ideas that were woven into this book.

HOWARD GLASSER

A few years back, a shared lunch at one of my seminars turned into a delicious conversation about the challenges and gains of resetting. What set this conversation apart was that it was in the company of three highly articulated and industrious Certified Nurtured Heart Approach Trainers who were discussing their individual and shared trials, tribulations and victories in striving to find the sweet spots of resetting. As a bystander to this riveting conversation, I found myself thinking, *this should be a book!* —and soon after I said this out loud, plans were being made to create the book you hold in your hands.

I am so deeply thankful to Lindsey Strasberg, Melanie Gretsch and Melissa Lowenstein Block for taking that ball and running with it. They have all poured their hearts, spirits, and wisdom into this volume and made this unfolding an awesome experience. I knew then and have confirmation now that this book will be a wonderful contribution to the Nurtured Heart Approach body of knowledge.

Thank you as well to Alice Glasser for her beautiful visual depictions of the processes we wished to communicate, and also for the cover art that we all immediately agreed was exactly what we were looking for. Your intuition and talents are exquisite and inspiring and it is such an honor to work with you and enjoy the greatness of endless admiration.

Finally, thank you to Owen DeLeon for translating the look of the inside pages to exactly the vehicle to convey our collective ideas into print. Your talents are immense and you are an absolute pleasure to work with. And the same is true for my friends in Hong Kong at Prolong Press - thank you!

ABOUT THE AUTHORS

MELANIE GRETSCH attended the University of Colorado at Boulder and earned her BA studying psychology. After graduating, Melanie became a personal shopper and created a vintage denim line. She enjoyed doing that for many years, until one day she opened her own clothing store. There, Melanie found a simple mission statement: to make people feel better about themselves when they leave than when they walked in. It was as though her years of studying psychology had found a home in helping people feel better about themselves and the way they dressed. She has stayed true to this mission.

After running the store successfully for over ten years, Melanie started her family. Finding it very hard to divide her time, she decided to sell her store and focus on raising her two girls. Melanie continued to study psychology, with a special focus on parenting. After some time, and after finding so much relief from reading and studying NHA, she created a support group for other mothers. Melanie is also the owner of a closet organizational company called Closet Sage—a way for her to continue to merge fashion and psychology by helping people to cleanse and purge things that no longer work and find special places for the things that do work.

LINDSEY STRASBERG is an entertainment lawyer and the mother of three teenagers. A graduate of NYU School of Law ('97) and partner at the Beverly Hills law firm Sloane, Offer, Weber and Dern. Lindsey considers herself a "lifestyle entrepreneur" who creatively structures her schedule to pursue a law practice, dedicate meaningful time to her husband, children and close friends, focus on her own personal evolution (especially in the area of parenting!), and pursue her other entrepreneurial passions. Recently, Lindsey entered a new arena, receiving her first credit as theatrical producer on the Broadway revival of the Tony-winning musical "Once on this Island."

MELISSA LOWENSTEIN, M.ED., is a writer, editor, non-profit professional, parent coach, and group facilitator. She holds a BA in Theater and Dance from the College of William and Mary in Virginia and a Master's in Education (with a concentration in Clinical Exercise Physiology) from the University of Virginia. Melissa has worked as a freelance writer and editor since 1997 and has authored, co-authored, and ghostwritten over 25 books on topics including education, psychology, parenting, relationships, social-emotional learning, intentional community, and health. She continues to write on these topics, publishing articles and blogposts with the intention of raising individuals' awareness and improving community well-being. Melissa is certified to teach and coach the Nurtured Heart Approach and has also been an actor, theater director, choreographer, contemporary dancer, and yoga teacher. She brings her parenting experience (parent to two, step-parent to three, born between the years of 2003 and 1993) and extensive personal work in compassionate communication, council, and conscious relationship to her work. She currently works full-time for AHA! (Attitude. Harmony. Achievement.), a non-profit that serves 3000+ teens per year with in-school and out-of-school programs, as Programs Coordinator and Core Facilitator; she also continues to write and publish on the Nurtured Heart Approach with its founder, Howard Glasser.

HOWARD GLASSER, creator of the Nurtured Heart Approach, is a psychotherapist, author, and Board Chairman of the Children's Success Foundation. He has authored 14 books including *Transforming the Difficult Child*, which remains a top seller on the topic of ADHD; and his most recent book, *Igniting Greatness*, which centers around applying the Nurtured Heart Approach to one's self as a way of transforming life and relationships. Howard spends much of his time providing trainings to parents, educators, treatment professionals, and those wishing to have transformative impact. He has been called the most influential living person working to have children free of medications and living lives of greatness. His work is currently being researched by Rutgers University and the University of Arizona, where he guest lectures at the School of Public Health, as well as at Dr. Andrew Weil's Integrative Medicine residency program.

Nurtured Heart Approach

Resources

Online Classes and Support

The Children's Success Foundation website, www.ChildrensSuccessFoundation.com, is the online learning center for the Nurtured Heart Approach. There, parents, educators, coaches and therapists can learn about the approach and then continually hone their expertise through innovative web courses, learning modules, discussion forums, and NHA-related research. The site also features articles, products and services supporting the approach.

Books on the Nurtured Heart Approach

Books can be ordered online through Amazon.com or through the Nurtured Heart Approach Bookstore at www.ChildrensSuccessFoundation.com. Phone orders can be made by calling our Distributor and Fulfillment Center, Brigham Distribution, at 415-723-6611.

Transforming the Intense Child Workbook
(2017) by Howard Glasser and Melissa Lowenstein

Transforming the Difficult Child: The Nurtured Heart Approach
(Revised 2016) by Howard Glasser and Jennifer Easley

All Children Flourishing—Igniting the Greatness of Our Children
(2008) by Howard Glasser with Melissa Lynn Lowenstein

Transforming the Difficult Child: True Stories of Triumph
(2008) by Howard Glasser and Jennifer Easley

ADHD Without Drugs — A Guide to the Natural Care of
Children with ADHD
(2010) by Sanford Newmark, MD

Notching Up the Nurtured Heart Approach — The New Inner
Wealth Initiative for Educators
(2011) Howard Glasser and Melissa Lynn Lowenstein

Igniting Greatness: Remembering Who We Really Are Through
the Nurtured Heart Approach
(2015) Howard Glasser and Melissa Lynn Lowenstein

AUDIO VISUAL RESOURCES

Transforming the Difficult Child DVD—(2004)
6 hours based on an actual filmed one-day seminar,
with video clip illustrations

Transforming the Difficult Child DVD—(2004)
4 hours based on an abbreviated version of the above

Transforming the Difficult Child CD—(2011)
3.5 hours recorded from a live seminar

Transforming the Difficult Child: The Nurtured Heart
Approach—Audio Book (2012)
by Howard Glasser and Jennifer Easley, read by Howard Glasser

Other titles by Nurtured Heart Approach trainers can be found at the
Nurtured Heart Approach bookstore.